Contents

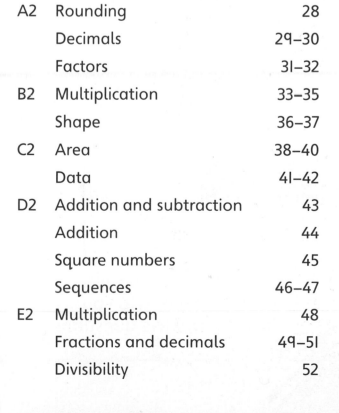

How to use this book

Speech bubbles raise interesting questions that you can discuss with others in your group.

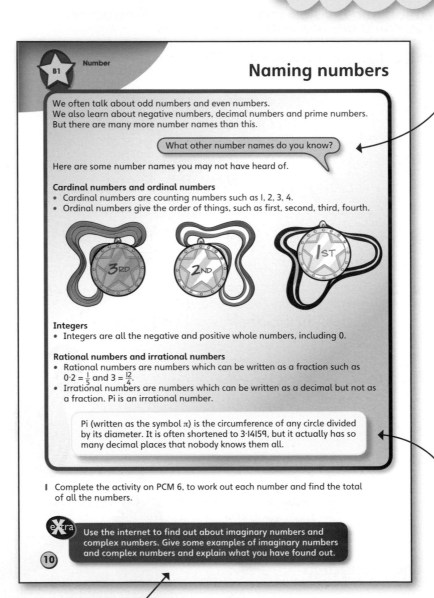

If you finish the main activity before the end of the lesson, you can move on to the Extra activity.

Yellow boxes give you useful tips to help you understand the questions.

What are you worth?

Look at the details of each coin on PCM I.

> Why do you think a 2p coin weighs twice as much as a Ip coin?
> Did you also notice that a I0p coin weighs twice as much as a 5p coin?

I For each coin, calculate the value of I000 coins.

2 For each coin, calculate the weight of I000 coins.

3 We could make piles of coins, placing one on top of the other.
For each coin, how high would a pile of I00 coins be?
What would be the value of each pile of I00 coins?

4 We could also lay coins out along a line, touching each other.
How far would I0 of each coin stretch?
Use this information to say how far I000 times more coins would reach.
Work out how far I million of each coin would reach.

> If I had my height in stacked £2 coins, I would have 580 £2 coins. What am I worth and how tall am I?

> If I had my weight in £2 coins, I would have 4I00 coins. What am I worth and how much do I weigh?

5 Solve this discussion. Which child is worth more?

Choose one type of coin. Which would you rather have, your weight in coins, your height in laid-out coins, or your height in stacked coins? Work out whether you would get more for your weight or for your height.

What is the total value of all the British coins in circulation?

3

Let's cook

Shortbread

Butter	$\frac{1}{3}$
Sugar	$\frac{1}{6}$
Flour	$\frac{1}{2}$

- Cream the butter and sugar.
- Add flour. Mix.
- Roll dough to 12 mm thick.
- Cut into strips.
- Bake for 15–20 mins at 190°C.

1 If Jo uses 300 g of flour, she can make 20 biscuits. How much butter and sugar does she need?

2 How much of each ingredient does she need to make 200 biscuits?

3 Jo has 300 g of butter. How much flour and sugar does she need? How many biscuits will she make?

4 To serve two people Ashraf uses 400 g of vegetables and 250 ml of stock. How much cream does he need (in ml)? How much onion (in grams)?

5 How much of each ingredient does Ashraf need to make soup for 20 people?

6 He has 2 kg of vegetables. How much of the other ingredients does he need? How many will it serve?

Vegetable soup

Oil for frying	
Chopped vegetables	0·4
Chopped onion	0·05
Stock	0·25
Cream	0·3
Seasoning	

- Fry onions and vegetables.
- Add stock and bring to boil.
- Simmer for 30 mins.
- Add cream and seasoning.

Pizza

Flour	50%
Butter	20%
Grated cheese	25%
Tomato puree	%
Splash of water	

- Mix flour and butter together.
- Add splash of water to form dough.
- Roll out dough.
- Spread with tomato puree. Sprinkle on cheese.
- Bake for 10 mins at 220°C.

7 What percentage of the pizza recipe is tomato puree?

8 If Monika uses 200 g of flour, the pizza will serve four. How much of the other ingredients does she need?

9 How much of each ingredient does she need to make a pizza for two?

10 Monika has 3 kg of flour. How much of the other ingredients does she need to use all this flour? How many pizzas for four can she make? How many people can she serve?

eXtra You are going to serve ten of your friends with this pizza. Write out the shopping list for the ingredients you will need.

Money for charity

Sunnyside School are raising money for their favourite charity.

Use the information on PCM I to work out the missing figures for each class.

1

Class 1

We have 100 identical coins that weigh 650 g in total.

They are coins.

Our coins are worth altogether.

2

Class 2

We have 100 identical coins that make a pile 17 cm high. The pile weighs 500 g.

They are coins.

Our coins are worth .

3

Class 3

We have 1000 identical coins that make a line 25·9 m long.

They are coins.

Our coins are worth .

4

Class 4

We have 1000 identical coins that weigh $3\frac{1}{3}$ kg in total.

They are coins.

Our coins are worth .

5

Class 5

We have 100 identical coins that make a pile 31·5 cm high.

They are coins.

Our coins are worth .

6

Class 6

We have 100 identical lines of coins. Each line has 100 identical coins. The lines are 203 m long in total.

They are coins.

Our coins are worth .

 How much money did the school raise in total? There are 200 children in the school. What was the average amount raised per child?

Casting out 9s

If a calculation has a whole-number answer, you can check it using the 'casting out 9s' method. It works for adding, subtracting, multiplying and dividing. This method came from India. It is often called the Hindu checking system. Arabian mathematicians brought it to Europe.

The 'casting out 9s' method should only be used to check answers, not to calculate them.

Addition

Check $3729 + 4861 = 8590$

Cross out any 9s and numbers that total 9.
Find the digit totals of the remaining numbers.
This number sentence is correct, so the calculation could be correct.

$$3729 + 4861 = 8590$$
$$3 + 1 = 4$$

Subtraction

Check $5326 - 2745 = 2581$

Cross out any 9s and numbers that total 9.
Find the digit totals of the remaining numbers.
This number sentence is correct, so the calculation could be correct.

$$5326 - 2745 = 2581$$
$$7 - 0 = 7$$

Multiplication

Check $536 \times 318 = 170448$

Cross out any 9s and numbers that total 9.
Find the digit totals of the two multipliers.
Multiply these together.
Find the digit total of the answer.
Find the digit total of the original answer.
The two digit totals match, so the calculation could be correct.

$$536 \times 318 = 170448$$
$$5 \quad \times \quad 3$$
$$5 \quad \times \quad 3 = 15$$
$$15 \rightarrow 6$$
$$170448 \rightarrow 24 \rightarrow 6$$

Division

Check $943 \div 23 = 41$

Cross out any 9s and numbers that total 9.
Find the digit totals of the numbers.
Multiply the last two digits of the number sentence.
Find the digit total of this number.
This digit total matches the digit total of the first multiplier, so the original answer could be correct.

$$943 \div 23 = 41$$
$$7 \div 5 = 5$$
$$5 \times 5 = 25$$
$$7$$

Use these methods to check the calculations on PCM 3.

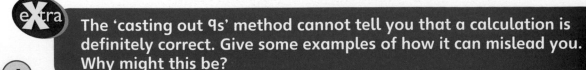

e**X**tra   The 'casting out 9s' method cannot tell you that a calculation is definitely correct. Give some examples of how it can mislead you. Why might this be?

How many are needed?

1 MP3 players are packed in boxes of 10. If 2455 MP3 players are packed, how many full boxes are there? Write the number left over as a decimal and a fraction.

2 Sonya works 84 hours in a month. How many 8-hour days does she work? Give the remainder as a fraction.

3 A large car holds five passengers. How many cars are needed to take 37 children on a school trip?

4 A table seats four children. There are seven classes, each with 30 children. How many tables does each class need? How many tables are needed altogether?

5 A minibus takes ten passengers. How many minibuses are needed for 114 passengers? How many spare seats will there be?

6 Party cakes come in packs of five. There are 212 children in a school. How many packs of cakes should be bought for a school party? What if the cakes came in packs of four? Or eight?

7 When Kulveer packs his apples in twos, fours, fives, eights or tens no apples are left over. He has more than 250 apples but less than 300. How many apples does he have?

8 Eight friends go for a meal. The bill is £145 and they share it evenly. How much does each person pay, to the nearest penny? If each person gives £20, will there be any change? How much?

9 David comes to visit from Canada. He brings 1007 Canadian dollars. The exchange rate is two Canadian dollars to one British pound. How much money does he have in pounds and pence?

10 Each car in a car factory needs 5 wheels. The factory has 456 wheels. How many cars can they make? They have an order to make 100 cars. How many more wheels do they need?

 eXtra

Jason works at a supermarket. He is paid £25·50 for 5 hours. How much does he earn in an hour? How much would he earn in 10 hours? 25 hours?

Jason is 16. Use the internet to find the minimum wage that he must be paid. How much above the minimum does he earn in 5 hours? 10 hours? 25 hours?

Consecutive numbers

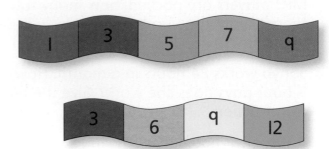

1 Which two consecutive counting numbers have a total of 3?

2 Which two consecutive odd numbers have a total of 4?

3 Which two consecutive even numbers have a total of 6?

4 Which three consecutive counting numbers have a total of 9?

5 Which four consecutive counting numbers have a total of 10?

6 Is it possible to make the numbers 1 and 2 by adding consecutive counting numbers, odd numbers or even numbers together?

7 Is it possible to make all the numbers from 3 to 20 by adding together two or more consecutive counting numbers, odd numbers or even numbers?

8 Look at the consecutive numbers in the 3 times table and the 5 times table. What numbers do you make by adding them?

I think that the smallest total you can make by adding consecutive multiples is always three times the start number. Do you think that is correct?

eXtra

If I add together three consecutive counting numbers I always get a multiple of 3 as my total. Does this always happen? Does it happen with odd and even consecutive numbers?
Do four consecutive numbers always total to a multiple of 4? What if they are odd or even numbers?
Do five consecutive numbers total a multiple of 5? What about six? Or seven?

Straw patterns

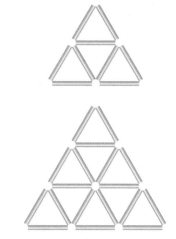

1 How many straws are used to make shape 1?

2 How many triangles have been made?

3 How many straws are used to make shape 2?

4 How many triangles have been made?

5 How many straws are used to make shape 3?

6 How many triangles have been made?

7 Complete the table up to shape 10 to show the numbers of straws used and triangles made. Use straws to make each shape yourself.

Shape	1	2	3	4	5	6	7	8	9	10
Triangular number	1	3	6							
Number of triangles	1	4	9							
Number of straws	3	9	18							

8 What number patterns can you see in your table?

9 Predict the numbers of straws and triangles for shapes 20 and 100.

10 What is the rule for the number of straws and triangles in shape n? How did you find this rule?

> To find the triangular number, add 1 to the shape number then multiply that by the shape number. Then divide the total by 2.

Look at these three patterns.

Draw up a table to find out how many straws you will need for the 10th pattern, the 20th pattern, the 100th pattern and the nth pattern.

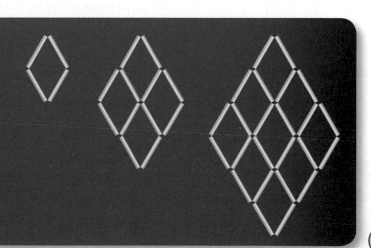

9

Naming numbers

We often talk about odd numbers and even numbers.
We also learn about negative numbers, decimal numbers and prime numbers.
But there are many more number names than this.

> What other number names do you know?

Here are some number names you may not have heard of.

Cardinal numbers and ordinal numbers
- Cardinal numbers are counting numbers such as 1, 2, 3, 4.
- Ordinal numbers give the order of things, such as first, second, third, fourth.

Integers
- Integers are all the negative and positive whole numbers, including 0.

Rational numbers and irrational numbers
- Rational numbers are numbers which can be written as a fraction such as $0·2 = \frac{1}{5}$ and $3 = \frac{12}{4}$.
- Irrational numbers are numbers which can be written as a decimal but not as a fraction. Pi is an irrational number.

> Pi (written as the symbol π) is the circumference of any circle divided by its diameter. It is often shortened to 3·14159, but it actually has so many decimal places that nobody knows them all.

1   Complete the activity on PCM 6, to work out each number and find the total of all the numbers.

eXtra Use the internet to find out about imaginary numbers and complex numbers. Give some examples of imaginary numbers and complex numbers and explain what you have found out.

Gate shapes

Find at least one of each of these 2D shapes in the photograph.
Use tracing paper to trace each shape that you find.

1 A rectangle

2 A rhombus

3 A parallelogram

4 A right angled triangle

5 An isosceles triangle

6 A small trapezium

7 A large trapezium

8 A small isosceles trapezium

9 A large isosceles trapezium

10 An irregular pentagon

11 An irregular hexagon

12 An irregular quadrilateral

 Find these features in the photograph and trace them

- A right angle
- An obtuse angle
- An angle of 60°
- An angle of 300°
- Three angles together making a straight line
- Two corresponding angles
- Four angles around a point
- An acute angle

- A reflex angle
- An angle of 120°
- Two angles together making a straight line
- Three different sets of parallel lines
- Two vertically opposite angles
- Two alternate angles
- Six angles around a point

Constructing triangles

Draw these four triangles using the measurements shown.

Measure all the angles.

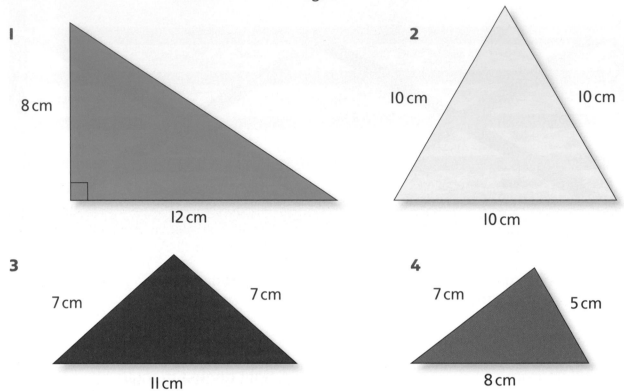

1

8 cm

12 cm

2

10 cm 10 cm

10 cm

3

7 cm 7 cm

11 cm

4

7 cm 5 cm

8 cm

eXtra

Some triangles are impossible to construct.
Try to construct these three triangles. Which one is impossible to construct? Why?

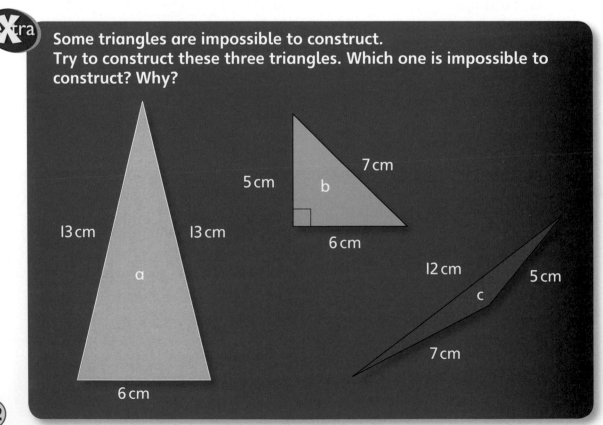

13 cm 13 cm

a

6 cm

5 cm 7 cm

b

6 cm

12 cm 5 cm

c

7 cm

Science test

This frequency table shows the scores of 200 children in a science test.

1–10	11–20	21–30	31–40	41–50	51–60	61–70	71–80	81–90	91–100
2	12	15	24	36	43	41	11	11	5

1 Draw a pictogram to represent these results. You will need to choose a suitable symbol and scale.

2 Describe the shape of the pictogram. How can you explain this?

3 What range of scores is the mode?

> The mode is the number that occurs the most.

4 What percentage of children scored more than 40? More than 70?

5 What percentage of children scored 50 or less? 80 or less?

6 What percentage of children scored between 21 and 70? 41 and 90?

7 What if the data were grouped into intervals of 20, such as 1–20, 21–40? Make a frequency table to show this. Draw a graph to represent the data.

8 What range of test scores is the mode now?

9 How does the shape of this graph compare to your first graph?

> What do you think the graph might look like if the same 200 children took the same test again, after a week of revision?

eXtra Redraw your graphs using a different scale and different symbols. What are the advantages and disadvantages of using the different scales?

13

Dice throws

Throw three dice.
Find the total of the three numbers.
You are going to do this 100 times.

> What totals can be made?

1 What do you think you will find out?

> Do you think all the possible dice totals will come up the same number of times?

2 Draw a tally chart to record your data. Throw three dice 100 times and record the totals in your chart.

3 Make a grouped frequency table for your data. Transfer the data from your tally chart to your frequency table.

> How will you group the data?

4 What type of graph will you draw to represent your data? Explain your choice.

5 Draw a graph of your data.

6 What does your graph show?

7 What total comes up most frequently?

8 How many times did you score 13 or more? 7 or more?

9 How many times did you score less than 9? Less than 15?

10 Write questions you could ask someone else about your graph.

11 What would happen to the shape of the graph if you threw the three dice another 100 times? Why?

e**X**tra What do you think you would find if you repeated the experiment using four dice instead of three? Test your predictions.

Metric lengths

How can you convert metres to centimetres?

10 mm = 1 cm
100 cm = 1 m
1000 m = 1 km

1 How many millimetres in 1 m?

2 How many centimetres in 1 km?

3 How many millimetres in 1 km?

4 Copy and complete this table showing the same lengths written in different units. The first row has been done for you.

Millimetres	Centimetres	Metres	Kilometres
1923	192·3	1·923	0·001923
	1720		0·0172
		623	
			23
	562		
4504			
		4217	
			7·2
	9500		
		78	

Write the following sets of lengths in order of size, smallest to largest:

5 235 cm, 2003 mm, 2·3 m

6 0·6 km, 607 m, 67 000 cm

7 99 000 mm, 9009 cm, 0·09 km

8 207 m, 7000 cm, 29 000 mm, 0·27 km

 Measure the length of your desk, your classroom and a book. Give each length in mm, cm, m and km.

A pound of carrots

EU imperial victory

Traders can continue using pounds and ounces following a campaign against European Union (EU) plans. The EU wanted to make the metric system compulsory, but this has been overthrown.

Pro-imperial organisations including the Metric Martyrs, who have been campaigning against being forced to use metric units, are delighted. The EU now say that imperial weights and measures can continue to be displayed alongside metric measures.

Campaigners in favour of the metric system think that keeping the dual labelling system is crazy!

1 kg = 2·2 lb
1 lb = 0·45 kg

Do you prefer measuring weight using metric or imperial units? Why?

Which is the best value in each case?

1 1 kg of bananas for 50p   or   1 lb of bananas for 25p

2 1 kg of oranges for 80p   or   1 lb of oranges for 35p

3 1 kg of tomatoes for £1·20   or   1 lb of tomatoes for 65p

4 1 kg of grapes for £2·55   or   2 lb of grapes for £2·30

5 3 kg of potatoes for £3·60   or   5 lb of potatoes for £2·80

6 2 kg of apples for £4·20   or   6 lb of apples for £7

7 1·5 kg of cherries for £6·40   or   4 lb of cherries for £8

8 3·5 kg of carrots for £3·90   or   2 lb of carrots for 90p

e**X**tra

Look at an old recipe book that uses imperial units.
Rewrite some of the recipes using metric units instead.

Imperial units

Length
  12 inches = 1 foot
    3 feet = 1 yard
  1760 yards = 1 mile

Weight
  16 ounces (oz) = 1 pound (lb)
    14 lb = 1 stone

1 How many inches in 16 feet?

2 How many inches in 9 yards?

3 How many yards in 7 miles?

4 How many feet in 3 miles?

5 How many ounces in 11 pounds?

6 How many pounds in 32 stone?

7 How many inches in a mile?

8 How many ounces in 3 stone?

Find the total of:

9 3 feet 5 inches and 4 feet 3 inches

10 7 feet 8 inches and 6 feet 9 inches

11 6 lb 7 oz and 3 lb 4 oz

12 3 lb 9 oz and 4 lb 12 oz

13 2 stone 3 lb and 9 stone 12 lb

Find the difference between:

14 7 feet 11 inches and 2 feet 6 inches

15 5 feet 2 inches and 3 feet 8 inches

16 9 lb 7 oz and 2 lb 3 oz

17 6 lb 4 oz and 3 lb 8 oz

18 9 stone 6 lb and 5 stone 10 lb

How tall are you in metres and centimetres?
How about feet and inches?

 eXtra Make up some questions similar to the ones above, but use only metric measures, such as metres and centimetres or kilograms and grams. What is different? Which system is easier? Why?

Angles around a circle

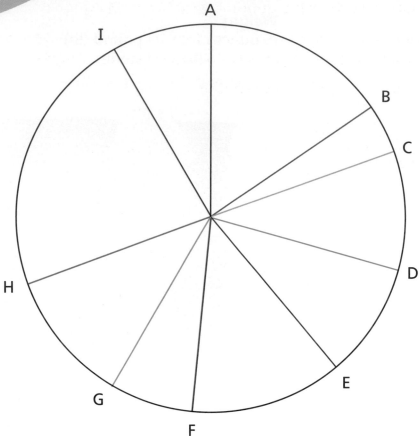

1 Measure the angle, in degrees, from A clockwise to each other line.

2 What would the angles be anticlockwise from A to each other line? Try to work them out without measuring.

3 Now you know the angle from A to B and the angle from A to D, what is the angle between B and D?

Use the method in question 3 to find the angle clockwise from:

4 B to E   **5** C to F   **6** E to G   **7** H to B   **8** H to C

9 B to G   **10** D to I   **11** F to B   **12** G to H   **13** I to E

Check your answers by measuring.

eXtra

Draw a circle and draw line N pointing north.
Draw the following lines clockwise from N: M 27°,
P 103°, Q 123°, R 200°, S 268° and T 312°.

Angles in quadrilaterals

Measure each angle in each of the quadrilaterals on PCM 13.

1 What can you say about opposite angles in a kite, a parallelogram and an isosceles trapezium? What can you say about consecutive angles?

2 Draw one more of each shape to check this.

3 Without measuring, find the missing angles in these shapes.

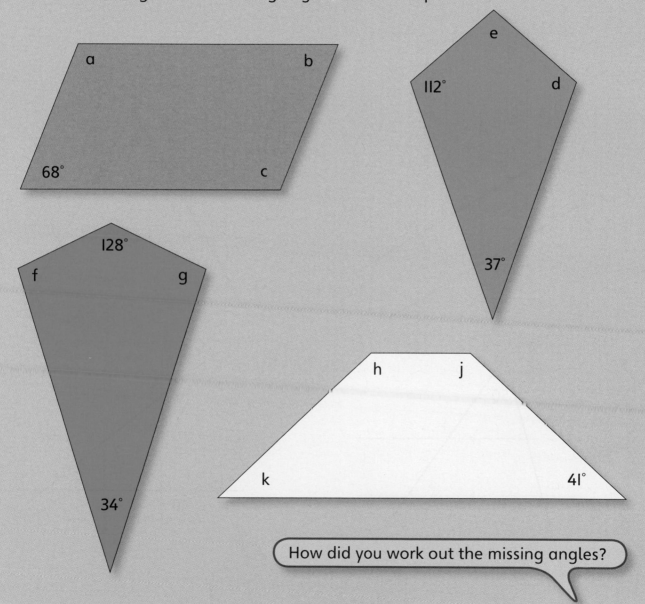

How did you work out the missing angles?

 eXtra Draw diagonals onto the shapes on PCM 13. What do you notice about the angles where the two diagonals cross? Investigate this for other quadrilaterals.

More missing angles

Find all the missing angles.

1

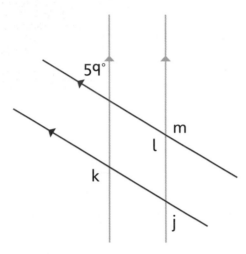

2

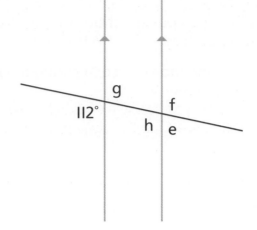

3

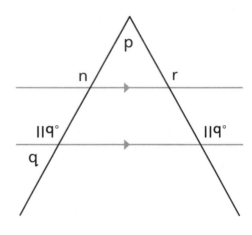

4

5

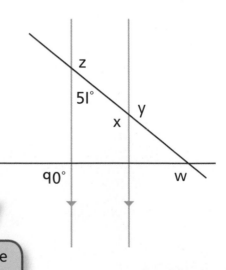

6

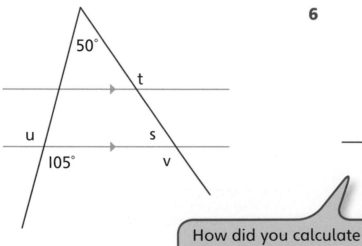

How did you calculate these angles?

Draw a set of three parallel lines with one, two or three lines crossing them. In each case, what is the minimum number of angles you must know in order to calculate all of the other angles?

Strange subtractions

1 Start with any 2-digit number with two different digits. Reverse the digits and subtract the smaller number from the larger number. Do this at least 10 times.

> **For example**
> Start with 25. Reverse and subtract. 52 – 25 = 27
> Start with 70. Reverse and subtract. 70 – 07 = 63

2 What do you notice about the answers?

3 Try it some more times to test out your hypothesis.

> Your hypothesis is the idea that you are investigating and trying to prove.

Was your hypothesis right?
Why do you think this happens?

4 Now investigate reversing and subtracting 3-digit numbers.

> **For example**
> Start with 371. Reverse and subtract. 371 – 173 = 198
> Start with 580. Reverse and subtract. 580 – 085 = 495

Does the same thing happen as with 2-digit numbers?

5 What do you think will happen with 4-digit numbers?

6 Try out your hypothesis, doing the subtractions mentally.

 Try this for 5-, 6- or 7-digit numbers. Does the same thing still happen?

Viewing figures

Top ten programmes in week ending 8 February 2009

			Millions
1	Cook with Confidence	(Wednesday 20:30)	4·69
2	Cook with Confidence	(Thursday 20:30)	4·635
3	Cook with Confidence	(Tuesday 20:30)	4·18
4	Celebrity Quiz	(Monday 20:00)	3·987
5	Back to School	(Thursday 20:15)	3·882
6	Heartbreak Road	(Tuesday 20:00)	3·75
7	Cook with Confidence	(Monday 20:30)	3·251
8	Living in the Wild	(Wednesday 21:00)	2·819
9	The Steve Clarke show	(Monday 19:00)	2·48
10	British Film Awards	(Sunday 20:00)	2·43

Find the difference between the numbers of viewers of these programmes.
Give your answers in both decimals and whole numbers.

1 *Back to School* and *The Steve Clarke Show*

2 *Celebrity Quiz* and the *British Film Awards*

3 *Cook with Confidence* on Wednesday and Thursday

4 *Cook with Confidence* on Monday and Tuesday

5 *Living in the Wild* and *Heartbreak Road*

True or false?

6 More people watched the four editions of *Cook with Confidence* than all of the other six programmes altogether.

7 Twice as many people watched Tuesday's *Cook with Confidence* as watched *The Steve Clarke Show*.

8 If twice as many people had watched the British Film Awards it would have been number 1 on the list.

9 More than half a million more people watched *Cook with Confidence* on Thursday as did on Tuesday.

10 Less than a quarter of a million more people watched *Living in the Wild* than *The Steve Clarke Show*.

eXtra Visit the BARB website and find the differences between some viewing figures for your favourite programmes or channels. Make up some true or false questions for other children to answer.

Last digits

Amy took a I-digit number and doubled it several times, like this:

$$3 \rightarrow 6 \rightarrow 12 \rightarrow 24 \rightarrow 48 \rightarrow 96 \rightarrow 192 \rightarrow 384$$

She listed the last digits in order, like this:

3   6   2   4   8   6   2   4

Amy's last digits make a repeating pattern:

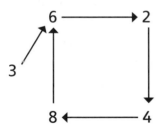

I Try this with your own I-digit number. What pattern do you see?
   Does your pattern continue?

2 Now try this with a negative number. What happens?

3 Try a 2-digit number. What do you find?

4 Why do you think this happens? Will it always happen?

eXtra Take a 2-digit number and follow these rules:
   • If it is even, halve it.
   • If it is odd, add 3.
   Write the answer each time. Carry on halving until you come to an end.
   Look at the last digits. What do you find? Is this what you expected?
   Why do you think this happens? Will it always happen?

Binary numbers

Binary numbers use only two different digits: Is and 0s. Binary numbers are sometimes called numbers in **base 2**. Our normal number system is called **denary** or **base 10**.

Computers work using the binary number system. The computer sees the numbers as electric signals. These are either 'on' or 'off'. Each I is 'on', and each 0 is 'off'.

II is a binary number. But it is not the same as our normal denary number II.

Look at the table. The headings show the value of each I.

128	64	32	16	8	4	2	1
						I	I
			I	I	0	0	0
			I	0	I	I	

II in binary is 2 + 1 = 3 in denary.

II 000 in binary is 16 + 8 = 24 in denary.

I0II in binary is 8 + 2 + 1 = II in denary.

Work out what these binary numbers are in denary.

I 10　　　　**2** 101　　　　**3** III　　　　**4** 1010　　　　**5** 10 000 001

For each of these denary numbers, write the binary number.

6 23　　　　**7** 54　　　　**8** II　　　　**q** 160　　　　**10** 200

e**X**tra Some binary numbers have special names. A binary number with 8 digits is called a **bit**.
- 4 bits is a **nibble**
- 8 bits is a **byte**
- 16 bits is a **word**
- 32 bits is a **double word**
- 64 bits is a **quad word**.

How many binary digits are there in a byte? How many binary digits are there are in a double word? Try to write your answers in both denary and in binary.

Russian multiplication

In the past, Russian peasants used two bowls of pebbles to help multiply.

They took pebbles from each bowl to match the numbers to be multiplied. They then halved one number and doubled the other. They continued until one number was reduced to I. This told them the product of the numbers.

For example: 18 × 6

Take 18 pebbles.
Put 9 pebbles back.
Put 4 pebbles back.
Put 2 pebbles back.
Put I pebble back.

Take 6 pebbles.
Take 6 more pebbles.
Take 12 more pebbles.
Take 24 more pebbles.
Take 48 more pebbles.

Halve		Double
18	×	6
9	×	12
4	×	24
2	×	48
I	×	96

If you have an odd number on the left, take away I then halve it.

After you have halved and doubled, cross out any rows where the left-hand number is even.

Then add together the numbers on the right that are not crossed out: 12 + 96 = 108

So 18 × 6 = 108.

Halve		Double
~~18~~	×	~~6~~
9	×	(12)
~~4~~	×	~~24~~
~~2~~	×	~~48~~
I	×	(96)

Try these calculations using the Russian method. Find an approximate answer first.

I 46 × 13

2 37 × 16

3 65 × 50

4 77 × 14

5 86 × 27

6 34 × 34

7 45 × 33

8 92 × 54

9 20 × 93

 eXtra You can use the Russian method to multiply whole numbers by decimals. Try these calculations. Remember to make an approximation first.

24 × 1·2   46 × 3·2   66 × 7·8

Egyptian fractions

The Ancient Egyptians used fractions in their mathematics. They only used **unit fractions**.

$\frac{1}{2}$, $\frac{1}{3}$, $\frac{1}{4}$, $\frac{1}{5}$ and $\frac{1}{6}$ are all unit fractions.

They have a 1 as the numerator.

The Egyptians wrote other fractions as the sums of unit fractions.

For example, they wrote $\frac{2}{3}$ as $\frac{1}{2} + \frac{1}{6}$.

> You can check this with equivalent fractions: $\frac{3}{6} + \frac{1}{6} = \frac{4}{6} = \frac{2}{3}$.

The Egyptians wrote $\frac{3}{5}$ as $\frac{1}{2} + \frac{1}{10}$.

> Check: $\frac{5}{10} + \frac{1}{10} = \frac{6}{10} = \frac{3}{5}$.

Which is bigger, $\frac{2}{3}$ or $\frac{3}{5}$?
With Egyptian fractions it's easy to tell.

$\frac{2}{3}$ is $\frac{1}{2}$ and $\frac{1}{6}$. $\qquad$ $\frac{3}{5}$ is $\frac{1}{2}$ and $\frac{1}{10}$

Both fractions have $\frac{1}{2}$, but $\frac{1}{6}$ is bigger than $\frac{1}{10}$ so $\frac{2}{3}$ must be bigger than $\frac{3}{5}$.

Use PCM 17 to compare the fractions below.
Draw a table like this to answer each question.

Fraction	Egyptian fraction	Bigger?	Reason
$\frac{2}{3}$	$\frac{1}{2} + \frac{1}{6}$	✓	Both have $\frac{1}{2}$. $\frac{1}{6}$ is bigger than $\frac{1}{10}$.
$\frac{3}{5}$	$\frac{1}{2} + \frac{1}{10}$		

1 $\frac{4}{9}$ and $\frac{1}{2}$

2 $\frac{2}{5}$ and $\frac{3}{8}$

3 $\frac{4}{7}$ and $\frac{5}{8}$

4 $\frac{2}{9}$ and $\frac{3}{10}$

5 $\frac{3}{10}$ and $\frac{2}{7}$

6 $\frac{5}{6}$ and $\frac{7}{10}$

7 $\frac{2}{5}$, $\frac{3}{8}$ and $\frac{4}{9}$

8 $\frac{3}{5}$, $\frac{2}{3}$ and $\frac{7}{10}$

9 $\frac{3}{4}$, $\frac{6}{11}$ and $\frac{5}{9}$

eXtra Use the internet to find out what you can about the Rhind Papyrus. Why was it important for understanding fractions? Write a report about what you find out.

Tides

As the tide went out, these were the water depths over six hours at a harbour wall.

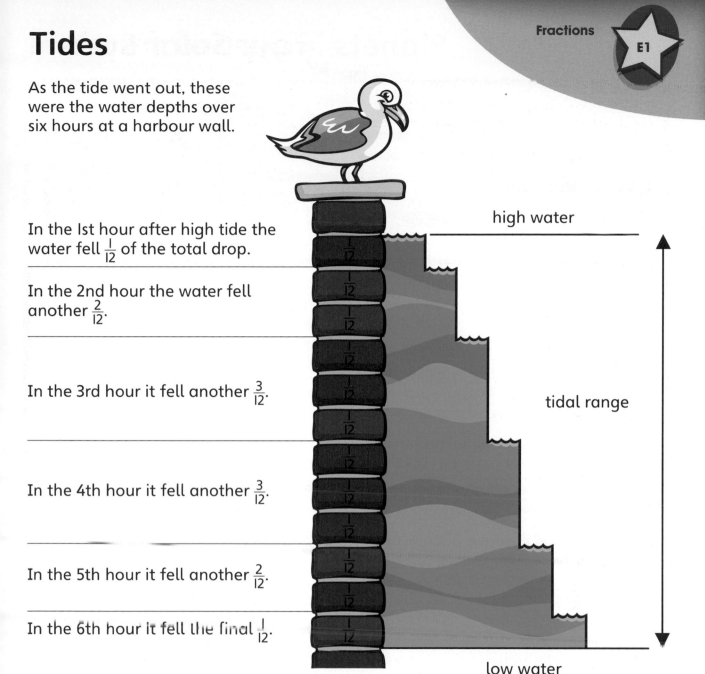

In the 1st hour after high tide the water fell $\frac{1}{12}$ of the total drop.

In the 2nd hour the water fell another $\frac{2}{12}$.

In the 3rd hour it fell another $\frac{3}{12}$.

In the 4th hour it fell another $\frac{3}{12}$.

In the 5th hour it fell another $\frac{2}{12}$.

In the 6th hour it fell the final $\frac{1}{12}$.

high water

tidal range

low water

This is the **rule of twelfths**. It works the same way when the tide comes in.

1 If high water is 12 m above low water, how much did the water fall in the first hour?

2 How much had it fallen after 5 hours?

3 Complete PCM 18.

At 12:40 the high water level was 3·6 m. At approximately 15:40 the water level was 2·4 m. Calculate approximately what the low water level would be and at what time it would occur. What would the water level be at approximately 14:40 and approximately 17:40?

Planets in our Solar System

According to scientists, our Solar System formed about 5 billion years ago. It started with a huge cloud of gas that formed planets and comets as it cooled. The gas ball in the centre of the cloud exploded in a huge nuclear reaction and became the Sun.

The eight planets of the Solar System rotate around the Sun. Ancient Greek astronomers noticed that the planets were constantly moving so they named them *planetes*, meaning wanderers.

In 2006 the International Astronomical Union officially classified Pluto as a dwarf planet, not a planet of the Solar System.

The table on PCM 19 shows information about the eight planets. It shows:
- the diameter of each planet
- its relative size to the Earth
- how long it takes to travel around the Sun.

> Watch out: some of the times are in years!

Complete the table:

1 Round each diameter to the nearest thousand kilometres.

2 Round each distance from the Sun to the nearest 10 million km.

3 Round each ratio to the nearest tenth.

4 Round each time to travel around the Sun to the nearest 100 Earth days.

eXtra

List the eight planets in order of size (diameter), beginning with the smallest.
Here are the planets in order of weight, beginning with the lightest:
Mercury, Mars, Venus, Earth, Uranus, Neptune, Saturn, Jupiter.
How does the order of planet size compare with the order of planet weight?

Which calculation?

£15 082 shared between 1000 children

£15 082 × 0·001

£15 082 × 0·1 × 0·01

£15 082 × 0·1 ÷ 10

£15 082 × 10 ÷ 0·0001

£15 082 × 10 × 0·0001

£15 082 ÷ 10 ÷ 10 ÷ 10

£15 082 ÷ 100 × 0·1

I Five of the calculations have the same answer. Which five? Write the answer in the middle of the first star on PCM 21. Write the five calculations around the points.

> You can use a calculator, but try to do each question mentally first.

2 Which two calculations do not give the same answer as the others? Why do they give different answers?

3 The circumference of the Earth is approximately 40 075 km. If you could run right around the Earth using a relay team of 10 000 runners, how far to the nearest metre would each person run?

4 The diameter of the Earth is 12 756 km. If you could run straight through the centre of the Earth using a relay team of 100 runners, what distance would each person run to the nearest 10 km?

 eXtra Find five different multiplications and divisions that all give the same answer as question 3. Look at the examples in question I for ideas. Use them to complete the second star on PCM 21.

Posting a parcel

 A 1·05 kg

 B 1·55 kg

 C 1995 g

 D 1505 g

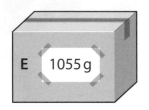 E 1055 g

1 Use the table below to calculate how much it will cost to post each of these parcels by Surface Mail

2 Use the table below to calculate how much it will cost to post each of these parcels by Air Mail

Weight up to	Surface	Air	Weight up to	Surface	Air
1050 g	£9·78	£11·67	1550 g	£14·29	£16·67
1100 g	£10·23	£12·07	1600 g	£14·74	£17·07
1150 g	£10·68	£12·67	1650 g	£15·17	£17·67
1200 g	£11·13	£13·07	1700 g	£15·60	£18·07
1250 g	£11·58	£13·67	1750 g	£16·03	£18·67
1300 g	£12·03	£14·07	1800 g	£16·46	£19·07
1350 g	£12·48	£14·67	1850 g	£16·89	£19·67
1400 g	£12·94	£15·07	1900 g	£17·32	£20·07
1450 g	£13·39	£15·67	1950 g	£17·75	£20·67
1500 g	£13·84	£16·07	2000 g	£18·18	£21·07

3 How much in total will it cost to send all five parcels by Surface Mail?

4 How much in total will it cost to send all five parcels by Air Mail?

5 How much could you save sending all the parcels by Surface Mail?

 e**X**tra

List the parcels in order of weight from lightest to heaviest. How much do the parcels weigh in total? Give your answer in both grams and kilograms.

Exploring powers of numbers

Look at the tables of numbers multiplied by themselves on PCMs 23 and 24.

1 Using a calculator, fill in the row for n = 4.

2 Fill in the rest of the numbers in row 10, and the first four numbers in row 7.

3 Fill in the columns for the squared and cubed numbers from 13 to 20.

4 Look at the final digit in each box in the columns. What do you notice?

5 What pattern can you see in the 5, 10, 15 and 20 rows? If you continued this table beyond 20, what numbers do you think would follow the same pattern?

6 What about the rows for 4 and 14? Or 6 and 16? Or 9 and 19?

7 What can you say about rows 5 and 6 and rows 15 and 16?

8 What do you notice about the numbers in the 2 and 20 rows?

9 Looking at rows 1 and 11, what digits do you think the numbers in rows 21 and 31 would end in?

10 Predict the last digit in the n^{11} and n^{12} columns for each number.

11 Look at the hundreds digit for row 5. What do you notice?

12 Can you see any other patterns in these numbers?

 On PCM 25 fill in the digital root of each number in the blank columns. Can you begin to predict the digital root before you work it out? What patterns did you use to make your predictions?

Horses in a field

Farmer Jones wants to make some paddocks for his horses. The paddocks are triangular. There is only room for one horse in each paddock. Each new paddock joins to the right hand side of the paddock before.

Fence strips are joined together at the ends with fasteners. The fasteners can join any number of fence strips together.

1 What is the smallest number of fence strips Farmer Jones can use for one horse?

2 How many strips does he need for two horses? For three horses?

3 Make a table like this to show how many fence strips and fasteners he would need for up to 10 horses.

Number of horses	Number of fence strips	Number of fasteners
1	3	3
2	5	4
3	7	5

4 How many fence strips would he need for 12 horses? For 20 horses? For *n* horses?

5 The farmer has 25 fence strips, and as many fasteners as he needs. How many paddocks can he make? How many fasteners does he need?

6 If he only has 12 fasteners, how many paddocks can he make?

7 Can he make complete paddocks using exactly 40 fence strips?

eXtra How many fence strips and fasteners would Farmer Jones need for each horse if the paddocks were square? Investigate the numbers of fence strips and fasteners needed to build different numbers of paddocks.

Where do the brackets go?

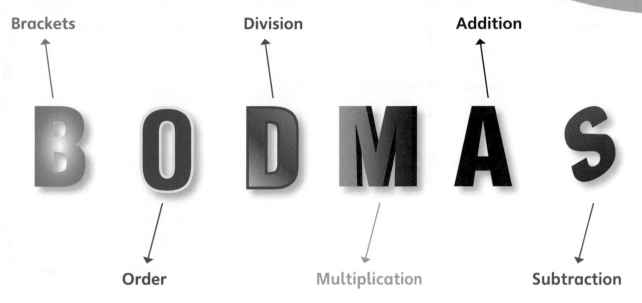

Brackets

Division

Addition

Order

Multiplication

Subtraction

The brackets have been left out of these calculations.
Where should the brackets go to make each calculation correct?

1 $48 \div 8 + 4 = 10$

2 $48 \div 8 + 4 = 4$

3 $23 + 46 \div 23 = 3$

4 $23 + 46 \div 23 = 25$

5 $36 \div 9 - 3 = 1$

6 $36 \div 9 - 3 = 6$

7 $25 - 19 + 45 \div 3 = 17$

8 $25 - 19 + 45 \div 3 = 21$

9 $30 + 20 \div 10 = 5$

10 $30 - 20 \div 10 = 28$

11 $28 - 7 \div 7 = 27$

12 $28 - 7 \div 7 = 3$

13 $140 \div 7 + 13 = 7$

14 $140 \div 7 + 13 = 33$

15 $36 + 36 \div 9 \times 20 = 160$

16 $36 + 36 \div 9 \times 20 = 800$

17 $38 \times 34 - 22 = 1270$

18 $38 \times 34 - 22 = 456$

19 $48 \div 4 + 44 = 56$

20 $48 \div 4 + 44 = 1$

eXtra Use a normal calculator and a scientific calculator to do the above calculations without brackets. What do you find?

Music maths

Do you know how a single or an album becomes Number 1?

The BPI represents the British music business. They collect data on music sales and work with The Official Charts Company to decide the chart ranking of each song and work out which is the most popular.

The BPI gives awards to their members which reflect the number of sales of singles and albums.

Award	Singles	Albums
Silver	Sales of 200 000 or more	Sales of 60 000 or more
Gold	Sales of 400 000 or more	Sales of 100 000 or more
Platinum	Sales of 600 000 or more	Sales of 300 000 or more

Here are the top five singles this week.

1 Did each single get a Silver award, a Gold award or a Platinum award?

	Title	Artist	Sales
1	Crazy About You	The Boyz	397 000
2	I Love Dancin'	Twin Thing	230 000
3	Shake It	Hip Star	226 000
4	Angel	Josh Lucas	190 000
5	Be Mine	Natalie Campo	184 000

Here are the top five albums this week.

	Title	Artist	Download sales	Total sales
1	At Night	The Kings	12·4%	220 929
2	Greatest Hits	The Cool Cats	4·1%	203 748
3	Magnet	Steel Style	6·8%	162 641
4	King of Hearts	Fernando	9·8%	155 861
5	Songs for You	Rachel James	2·6%	144 272

2 Did each album get a Silver award, a Gold award or a Platinum award?

3 Calculate the number of download sales for each album.

Use the internet to find out how many singles your favourite band sold last year. What percentage were download sales? How many singles was that?
Compare the Top 100 singles chart with the Top 40 download chart. Are they the same? Why?

Approximate multiplications

$5·6 \times \boxed{} = 36$

How could you find an approximate answer to this calculation?

You know that $6 \times 6 = 36$. So the missing number in the calculation must be more than 6, but close to it.

First attempt: **$5·6 \times 6·5 = 36.4$**   36·4 is too high.

Second attempt: **$5·6 \times 6·4 = 35·84$**   35·84 is too low. The missing number must be between 6·4 and 6·5.

Third attempt: **$5·6 \times 6·45 = 36·12$**   36·12 is a bit too high.

Fourth attempt: **$5·6 \times 6·43 = 36·008$**   36·008 is still a bit high.

Fifth attempt: **$5·6 \times 6·42 = 35·952$**   35·952 is a bit too low. 36·008 is closer than 35·952.

The missing number is **6·43**, to two decimal places.

We can check how close this answer is by dividing $36 \div 5·6$ on a calculator.

6.4285714

Find the missing numbers in these calculations, to two decimal places.
Use what you know about square numbers.
You will need to use a calculator to test each attempt!

1 $4·2 \times \boxed{} = 16$ **2** $7·6 \times \boxed{} = 49$ **3** $8·9 \times \boxed{} = 81$

Find the missing numbers in these calculations, to three decimal places.

4 $9·7 \times \boxed{} = 100$ **5** $5·3 \times \boxed{} = 25$ **6** $7·8 \times \boxed{} = 64$

7 $3·5 \times \boxed{} = 9$ **8** $1·9 \times \boxed{} = 4$ **9** $11·7 \times \boxed{} = 121$

 e**X**tra   **Write some numbers that are close to square numbers. Can you find their square roots, to two decimal places?**

Bird's eye view

Use six cubes to make each shape before you answer the question.
Match each view to the direction. Is it from the top, the front or the right?

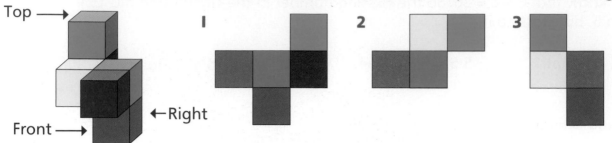

Top →

Front →

← Right

1 **2** **3**

4 Which of these are impossible views for this shape?

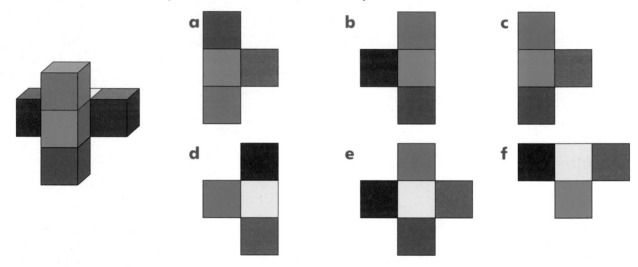

a **b** **c**

d **e** **f**

5 Only one shape matches all these views. Which shape is it?

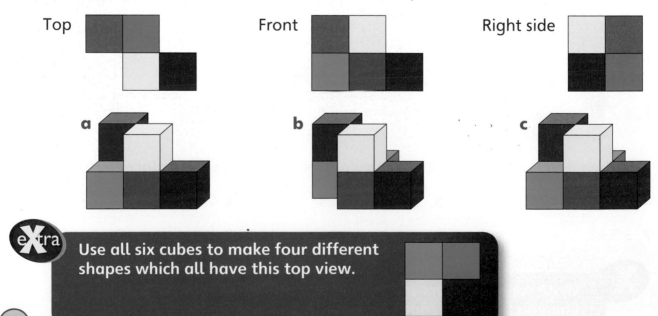

Top Front Right side

a **b** **c**

eXtra

Use all six cubes to make four different
shapes which all have this top view.

Seeing shapes

This picture is from the Scottish Parliament building in Edinburgh.

Find and trace these shapes in the picture.

You might have to look very closely to find some of them!

1 Two different-sized trapezia with the same size angles

2 A trapezium which is taller than it is wide

3 A pentagon

4 A parallelogram

5 A right-angled triangle

6 Two sides perpendicular to each other

7 Two faces perpendicular to each other

8 Two lines parallel to each other

9 An obtuse-angled triangle.

10 Two different acute, obtuse and reflex angles

 Look around the classroom from where you are sitting. What shapes can you see? Sketch them and describe them using the words on PCM 27.

Compound shapes

Which of these four shapes do you think has the greatest area?

I Find the area of each shape in at least two different ways. Explain your methods.

The shapes are not drawn to scale.

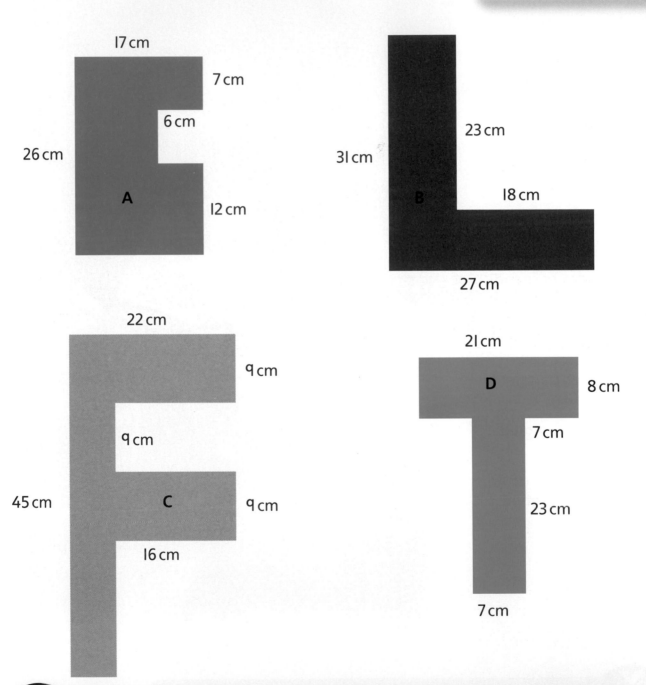

17 cm

7 cm

6 cm

26 cm

A

12 cm

23 cm

31 cm

B

18 cm

27 cm

22 cm

9 cm

9 cm

C

9 cm

45 cm

16 cm

21 cm

D

8 cm

7 cm

23 cm

7 cm

 e**X**tra Try making E, F, L and T shapes with areas between 200 and 250 cm².

Cuboid boxes

What is the difference between surface area and volume?

Find the surface area and volume of each box.

1

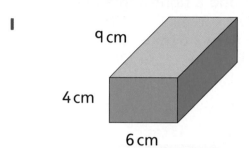

9 cm
4 cm
6 cm

2

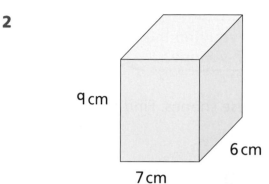

9 cm
6 cm
7 cm

3

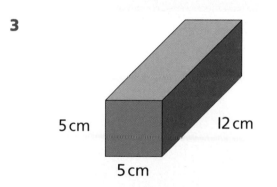

5 cm
12 cm
5 cm

4

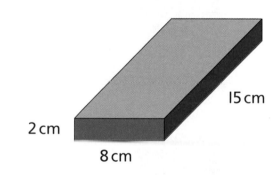

15 cm
2 cm
8 cm

5

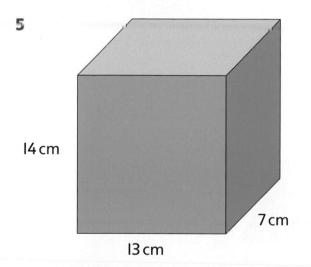

14 cm
7 cm
13 cm

6

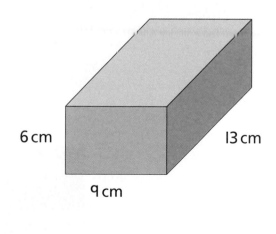

6 cm
13 cm
9 cm

 eXtra Find the surface area and volume of a 6 cm cube. What do you notice? What happens with cubes smaller or larger than this?

More compound shapes

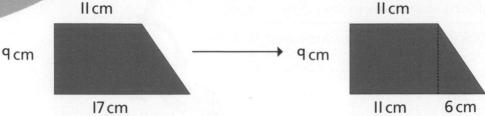

11 cm

9 cm

17 cm

⟶

11 cm

9 cm

11 cm   6 cm

How can you find the area of this shape?

Split it into a rectangle and a right-angled triangle:
Area of rectangle is 11 cm × 9 cm = 99 cm²
Area of triangle is $\frac{1}{2}$ of 9 cm × 6 cm = 27 cm²
So total area is 99 cm² + 27 cm² = 126 cm²

1 Copy these shapes. Find the area of each one.

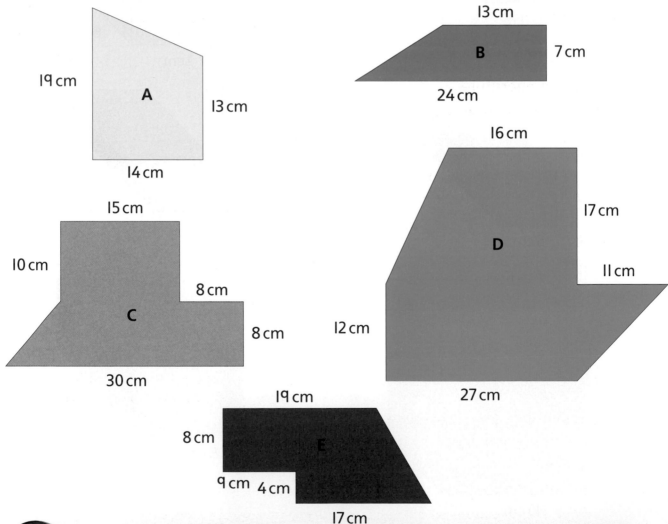

19 cm

A

13 cm

14 cm

13 cm

B

7 cm

24 cm

16 cm

17 cm

D

11 cm

12 cm

27 cm

15 cm

10 cm

8 cm

C

8 cm

30 cm

19 cm

8 cm

E

9 cm 4 cm

17 cm

Finding averages

Temperatures in °C during five days in May

City	Mon	Tue	Wed	Thu	Fri
Exeter	17	20	22	23	18
London	15	18	21	20	19
Birmingham	14	17	19	16	17
Cardiff	15	18	18	20	17
Manchester	13	19	19	15	16
Sheffield	12	18	19	14	17
Belfast	16	16	17	15	16
Glasgow	10	15	16	13	15

1 For each day find the:
- mean temperature
- mode temperature
- median temperature
- range of temperatures.

2 Which day had:
- the highest mean temperature?
- the highest mode temperature?
- the highest median temperature?
- the greatest range of temperatures?
- the lowest mean temperature?
- the lowest mode temperature?
- the lowest median temperature?
- the smallest range of temperatures?

> Which city had the highest temperature of the week?

3 On Wednesday the temperature in Liverpool was 19°C and in Aberdeen it was 14°C. If you included this information in your calculations, how would it affect the mean, mode, median and range of temperatures for Wednesday?

 Which city has the highest mean temperature? Which city has the highest mode? Which city has the highest median? Which city has the lowest mean temperature? Which city has the lowest mode? Which city has the lowest median?

Conversion graphs

Converting inches to centimetres

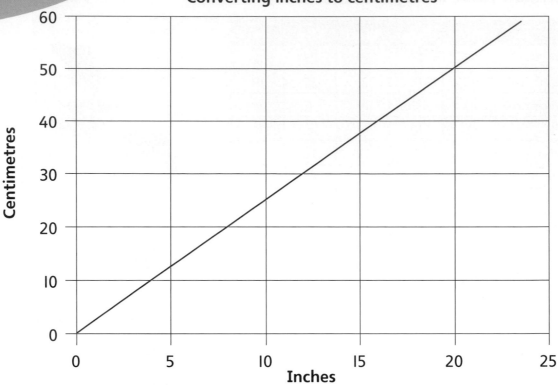

Use the graph to find out how many centimetres are equal to:

1 5 inches   **2** 20 inches   **3** 12 inches   **4** 7 inches

Use the graph to find out how many inches are equal to:

5 10 cm   **6** 50 cm   **7** 35 cm   **8** 23 cm

> How could you find the number of centimetres in 30 inches?

9 Use a calculator to find more accurate answers to questions 1–8.

> 1 inch = 2·54 cm

10 How different are the accurate answers from the ones you read from the graph?

11 Why are the answers from the graph not as accurate?

12 Draw a conversion graph between miles and kilometres.

> 1 mile = 1·6 km

eXtra   Use the internet to make your own conversion graphs exploring the relationships between imperial and metric measures of weight.

Adding decimals

1 Copy and complete the grid.

+	1·5	3·7	0·52	10·37			5·012
2·09					18·53		
7·1						14·2	
3·2				4·9			
	12·62						
				11·31			
			7·21				
	9·22						
							11·11

2 Check six of your answers using the inverse operation.

3 Find the total of the numbers in each column.
Which column has the largest total?
Mark it on your grid with a ★

4 Find the total of the numbers in each row.
Which row has the largest total?
Mark it on your grid with a ✓

How could you find the total of all the numbers in the grid without adding all 64 answers individually? What is the total of all the numbers in the grid?

Dinner out

1 Estimate the total cost of each bill below using the menu on PCM 29.
Which bill do you think is largest?

A | Abacus Restaurant
123 Maths Street

Date: May 04 2010   Time: 21:00

1	PRAWN COCKTAIL
1	SEAFOOD SALAD
1	RACK OF RIBS
1	LAMB CUTLETS
1	GARLIC BREAD
1	FRUIT SALAD
1	APPLE PIE AND CREAM
1	LEMONADE
1	SPARKLING WATER

Total

B | Abacus Restaurant
123 Maths Street

Date: May 04 2010   Time: 21:00

1	MUSSELS
1	SARDINES
1	CHEF'S SPECIAL
1	DUCK WITH ORANGE
1	SALMON
1	RICE
2	CHIPS
1	ICE CREAM
1	CHOCOLATE SPONGE
1	FRESH APPLE JUICE
1	FRESH ORANGE JUICE

Total

C | Abacus Restaurant
123 Maths Street

Date: May 04 2010   Time: 21:00

1	THREE COLOURED SALAD
1	PINK PRAWNS
1	SPAGHETTI WITH BACON
1	CAJUN CHICKEN
1	MIXED SALAD
2	CRÈME CARAMEL
2	DIET COLA

Total

D | Abacus Restaurant
123 Maths Street

Date: May 04 2010   Time: 21:00

1	HAM AND MELON
1	TUNA AND BEAN SALAD
1	GRILLED CHOP
1	SIRLOIN STEAK
1	SCAMPI
3	CHIPS
2	LEMONADE
1	MIXED FRUIT CRUSH

Total

2 Now work out the exact prices.
Check using a calculator.

Were your estimates close?

3 Choose a meal for yourself and a friend and find the total cost.

What methods did you use for adding the prices in your head?

e**X**tra

Between 3 o'clock and 8 o'clock on Saturday the restaurant offers a
10% discount. What would each of the bills cost during that time?

Square roots

Number	Square root
1	
4	
9	
16	
25	
36	
49	
64	
81	
100	
121	
144	
169	
196	
225	

1 Copy and complete the square root table.

Samira and Sean are investigating square roots.

What do you think the square root of 40 is?

6 squared is 36 and 7 squared is 49, so it's between 6 and 7. Let's try 6·5. **42·25**. That's too high. Let's try 6·4. **40·96**. Still too high. Let's try 6·3. **39·69**. Now it's too low! Let's try 6·35.

40·3225. Too high! Let's try 6.33. **40·0689**. Still too high. Let's try 6·32. **39·9424**. That's too low. My last guess is 6·325.

40·005 625. That's close enough!

Use this method to find a close approximation for the square roots of:

2 22   **3** 75   **4** 112   **5** 6   **6** 212

e^xtra Use the information in your table to draw a line graph showing numbers and their squares. Use your graph to find approximate square roots for other numbers.

Brackets

If you do a series of operations in a different order, how does it affect the answer?

If you see brackets, you do the operation inside them first.

> $3 \times (6 + 7) = 3 \times 13 = 39$ **but**
> $(3 \times 6) + 7 = 18 + 7 = 25$

Which gives the bigger result in each case?

1 $5 \times (3 + 8)$ or $(5 \times 3) + 8$

2 $40 \div (10 - 2)$ or $(40 \div 10) - 2$

3 $8 \times (23 - 2)$ or $(8 \times 23) - 2$

4 $9 + (17 \times 3)$ or $(9 + 17) \times 3$

5 $7 \times (6 - 3)$ or $(7 \times 6) - 3$

Which of these will give the bigger answer?
$(6 \times 11) - 5 \times 8$ or $6 \times (11 - 5) \times 8$ or $6 \times 11 - (5 \times 8)$

Investigate the effect of putting a pair of brackets in different places in these calculations. What different answers can you get for each calculation?

6 $12 \times 6 \div 3 + 9 =$

7 $11 + 3 \times 4 + 7 =$

8 $8 \times 9 - 3 \times 5 =$

9 $52 \div 4 + 9 \times 5 =$

10 $21 + 35 \times 6 - 2 =$

eXtra Try using the numbers 52, 10, 26 and 13, any two different operations and one pair of brackets. What is the largest result? What is the smallest?

Matchstick patterns

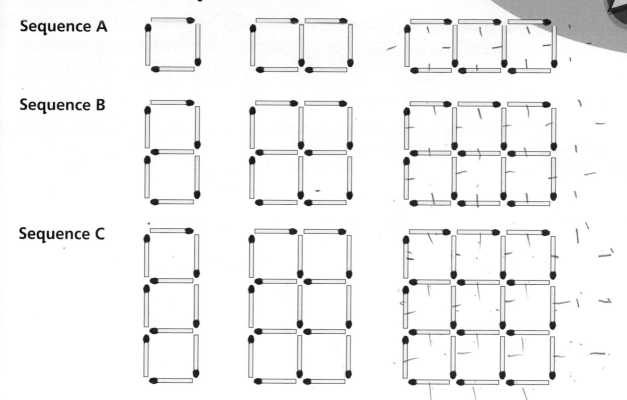

Sequence A

Sequence B

Sequence C

In sequence A you need 4 matchsticks for the first pattern, 7 matchsticks for the second pattern and 10 matchsticks for the third pattern.

1 How many matchsticks would you need for each of the patterns in sequence B? Sequence C?

2 For each sequence A, B and C draw the next two diagrams. How many matchsticks would you need for each?

3 Copy and complete this table to show what you have found.

	1st pattern	2nd pattern	3rd pattern	4th pattern	5th pattern
Sequence A	4	7	10		
Sequence B					
Sequence C					

4 For each sequence A, B and C, how many matchsticks would there be in the 10th pattern?

> What information did you use to make your predictions?

 Sequence D begins with four joined squares and sequence E begins with five joined squares. How would these sequences continue? Estimate, using the patterns you have found, before drawing the sequences.

Bestselling books

End of year bestseller list

Position	Title	This week's sales	Total sales for the year	Cost per book
1	*Tony's Tall Tale*	24 235	136 745	£3·99
2	*New Ends*	21 450	209 125	£4·00
3	*Surprise!*	19 470	152 100	£4·99
4	*Mountain Track*	16 455	75 200	£6·00
5	*Wet Weekend*	11 215	110 455	£7·00
6	*Hillside*	9070	140 560	£7·99
7	*Down Down*	8695	127 535	£5·99
8	*Two Together*	6985	101 275	£2·99
9	*Sky Blue*	6105	87 140	£8·00
10	*Madge and Mike*	5920	36 465	£9·99

1 This week, how many more copies of *Tony's Tall Tale* were sold than *Madge and Mike*?

2 Taking all the books in this list, how many books were sold this week?

3 How many copies of *Down Down* were sold this year before this week?

4 Meera says, in total, more than 2 000 000 of the books in the list were sold during the year. Can she be correct?

5 Marc says that, for most books, at least 10% of their total sales were sold this week. Is he right?

6 Dan says the average cost of the 10 books in the list is approximately £6. Is he correct?

7 What is the value of this week's sales for the book that sold the most copies this week plus the book that sold the fewest copies this week?

8 Paula says the number 1 book this week made more money in total over the year than any other book in the list. Is this true?

9 List the books in order of total value of sales over the year.

10 Eva thinks the total value of all the books sold over the year is approximately £6 000 000. Is she right?

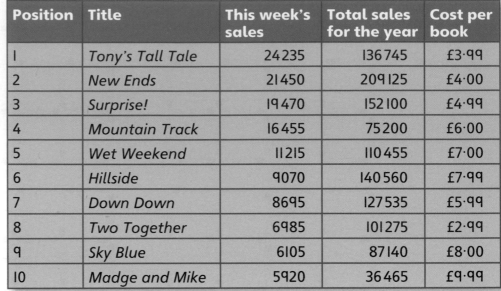

eXtra

If all books were reduced by £1·00 for this week only, how much less money was made per title this week?

Food guidelines

The first table shows the amounts of some nutrients a woman should eat each day.

The tables below show what percentage of the total recommended daily amount each food gives.

Calculate the missing figures.
Round percentages to the nearest whole number.
If the percentage is less than 0·5%, write 0%.

Calories (kcal)	2000
Sugars (g)	90
Fat (g)	70
Saturated fat (g)	20
Salt (g)	6

1 Pizza (180 g serving)

Calories (kcal)	460	23%
Sugars (g)	4	4%
Fat (g)	19	27%
Saturated fat (g)		40%
Salt (g)	2	33%

2 Coleslaw (100 g serving)

Calories (kcal)		4%
Sugars (g)	9·8	11%
Fat (g)	0·6	1%
Saturated fat (g)	0·2	1%
Salt (g)	0·2	4%

3 Oats (40 g serving)

Calories (kcal)		8%
Sugars (g)	0·5	1%
Fat (g)	3·6	
Saturated fat (g)	0·7	3%
Salt (g)	0	0%

4 Pasta with sauce (200 g serving)

Calories (kcal)	193	
Sugars (g)	6·5	7%
Fat (g)	17·9	
Saturated fat (g)	2·3	12%
Salt (g)	1	17%

5 Mixed vegetables (100 g serving)

Calories (kcal)	49	
Sugars (g)	0	0%
Fat (g)	2·8	4%
Saturated fat (g)	1·1	6%
Salt (g)	0·8	13%

6 Bacon (20 g serving)

Calories (kcal)	319	
Sugars (g)		10%
Fat (g)	8·0	11%
Saturated fat (g)	1·5	8%
Salt (g)	1·6	27%

7 Cornflakes (30 g serving)

Calories (kcal)		6%
Sugars (g)	2·5	3%
Fat (g)	0·3	0%
Saturated fat (g)	0·1	0%
Salt (g)	0·5	

8 Milk (200 ml serving)

Calories (kcal)		5%
Sugars (g)	0·5	1%
Fat (g)	6·1	
Saturated fat (g)	4·1	21%
Salt (g)	0·3	4%

eXtra Choose what Mrs Boronski might eat, in one day, from these choices. Would this give her the recommended daily amounts of all these nutrients?

It is important for drivers to know how much petrol they will need to travel a certain distance. Petrol is burned in a car engine to produce energy and make the car move. As the petrol is burned up, drivers need to fill their cars up with more petrol.

Burning petrol is expensive and bad for the environment, so people are designing 'green cars' that cause less damage to the environment. They run on other sources of energy, such as electricity, hydrogen, or even solar energy from the Sun.

Answer these questions using the information on PCM 31.

Give amounts of fuel in both litres and gallons, and give distances in both miles and kilometres.

> 4·5 litres = 1 gallon
> 1·6 kilometres = 1 mile

1 Which car has the biggest proportion of its tank full of petrol?

2 For each car calculate the proportion of its fuel tank that is empty.

3 Which car can hold the most fuel in its tank?

4 Which car has the most fuel in its tank at the moment?

5 How much fuel does each car need in order to fill up?

6 If petrol costs 85p per litre, how much would it cost to fill up each car?

7 How much will the total fuel bill be for all the cars to fill up?

8 How much petrol would all the cars hold in total, if all tanks were full?

9 Which car is the most economical? (This is the one that can go the furthest on one litre of petrol.)

10 All the cars start from the same place, with the amounts of fuel shown on the PCM. Which car can go furthest before running out of petrol?

eXtra

If all the petrol tanks are full and all the cars start from the same place, which car can go furthest before running out of petrol?
Add together the total distance each car can go on one full tank of fuel. What is the total? Give your answer in miles and kilometres.

Magazine monthly

Here are the magazines that some children from Class 6b buy.

	How often published	As a fraction of a year	As a decimal (2 d.p.)	Cost per copy	Total cost per year
Baljit *Fashion Focus*	Quarterly	$\frac{1}{4}$	0·25	a	£47·80
Ricky *Today's Gamer*	Biannual	b	c	£17·99	d
Louisa *Sport and Health*	e	f	0·17	£6·85	£41·10
Jamal *On the Ball*	Every 4 months	$\frac{1}{3}$	g	£14·05	h
Sadie *Sci-fi Dimensions*	i	$\frac{1}{12}$	0·83	j	£52·20
Kezia *Star Gossip*	Weekly	k	l	£0·92	m
Jonah *My Music*	n	$\frac{1}{26}$	0·04	o	£45·50
Marta *Really Wild Animals*	Every 4 weeks	p	0·08	£3·99	q

I Work out each missing piece of information.

2 Who pays the most each year?

3 Who do you think gets the best value? Why do you think this?

4 What is the total number of magazines bought by these eight children over a year?

eXtra The children pay for these magazines out of their weekly pocket money. How much does each person have to save each week to pay for their magazines?

Square number patterns

Josh and Samir are talking about dividing square numbers.

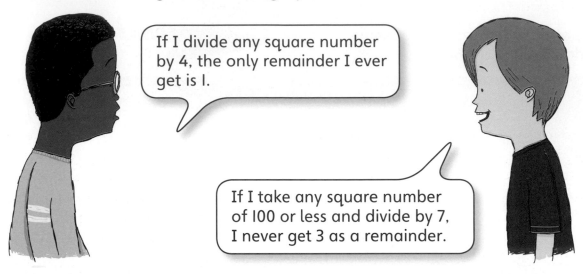

If I divide any square number by 4, the only remainder I ever get is 1.

If I take any square number of 100 or less and divide by 7, I never get 3 as a remainder.

1 Prove whether or not Josh and Samir are correct. Are they correct for square numbers bigger than 100?

Alina and Leila found something interesting too.

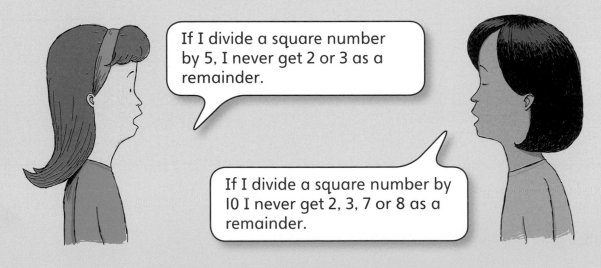

If I divide a square number by 5, I never get 2 or 3 as a remainder.

If I divide a square number by 10 I never get 2, 3, 7 or 8 as a remainder.

2 Prove whether or not Alina and Leila are correct. Are they correct for square numbers bigger than 100?

e**X**tra Explore dividing square numbers by other single digits. What patterns do you see? Do any two single digits give similar results?

Flying high

> Heat rises, and the top of a mountain is closer to the Sun. So why is it colder at the top of a mountain than at the bottom?

The Sun is 93 000 miles away. This is a huge distance, so even if you climbed a mountain 6 miles high, the Sun would make no difference to the temperature. The thing that does make a difference is the air pressure. Air pressure decreases as the altitude (height) increases, and this makes the temperature fall.

Altitude in feet	Air pressure in pounds per square inch (PSI)	Altitude in metres	Air pressure in Newtons per square cm (N/cm²)
0 (sea level)	14·7	0 (sea level)	10·14
10 000	10·2	3048	7·03
20 000	6·4	6096	4·41
30 000	4·3	9144	2·96
40 000	2·7	12 192	1·86
50 000	1·6	15 240	1·1

The temperature outside an aeroplane depends on how high it is flying. At cruising height the air outside is very cold.

The temperature of the air falls about 6·5°C for every kilometre above the ground. So at 10 km up, a common cruising height, the temperature is approximately 65°C colder than it is on the ground.

Complete PCM 36.

Use the internet to find out more about:
- Vijaypat Singhania, who holds the world record for the highest hot air balloon flight. How high did he fly? What was the air pressure at his highest point? Can you find out the temperature?
- Steve Fossett, who holds the record for the highest glider flight. How high did he fly? What was the air pressure at his highest point? Can you find out the temperature?

The rate of VAT in the UK changed from
17·5% to 15% in December 2008.

Here is a quick way of calculating VAT at 17·5%:
Find 10% of the price. Then halve that to find 5%. Then halve again
to find 2·5%. Add up the 10%, 5% and 2·5% to find the total VAT.

For example:

Price of sweatshirt	£20·00
10%	£ 2·00
5%	£ 1·00
2·5%	£ 0·50
Total cost with VAT	£23·50

1 What would be the total cost of the £20 sweatshirt with VAT at 15%?

For each of these items calculate the price with VAT at 17·5% and 15%.

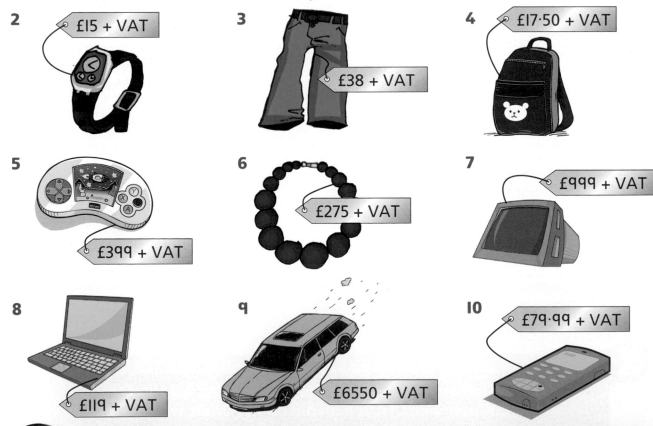

2 £15 + VAT

3 £38 + VAT

4 £17·50 + VAT

5 £399 + VAT

6 £275 + VAT

7 £999 + VAT

8 £119 + VAT

9 £6550 + VAT

10 £79·99 + VAT

eXtra How much do you save on each item if VAT changes from 17·5% to 15%?
How much do you save for all the items together?
How much would you save for all the items if the VAT rate fell to 12·5%?

Stretching and shrinking

> We are taller at the beginning of the day than at the end! Why?

How tall would these people be at night if they shrank 0·5% during the day?

1 Sally is 1·56 m tall when she wakes up.

2 Akash is 145 cm tall when he gets up.

3 Jo is 1·95 m in the morning.

4 Satvinder is 1350 mm when he gets up.

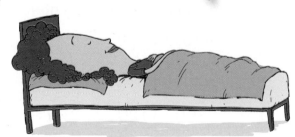

> Why are steel bridges taller on a warm day than on a cold day?

Golden Gate Bridge

How tall would these bridges be if their height increased by 0·15%?

5 Sydney Harbour Bridge 134 m high

6 Golden Gate Bridge 227 m high

7 Forth Road Bridge 156 m high

8 Humber Bridge 155·5 m high

> Why do clothes shrink if you wash them at too high a temperature?

Work out the new length after each washing disaster.

9 A jumper that was 65 cm long shrank by 20%.

10 Trousers that were 75 cm long shrank by 10%.

11 A shirt that was 0·45 m long shrank by 22%.

12 A skirt that was 54 cm long shrank by 30%.

eXtra

Sometimes clothes stretch when they are washed in hot water. Work out the new length after each washing disaster.
- A jumper that was 65 cm long stretched by 10%.
- Trousers that were 75 cm long stretched by 5%.
- A shirt that was 0·45 m long stretched by 50%.
- A skirt that was 54 cm long stretched by 25%.

Messy maths book

Find the mistakes and missing numbers. Check if each answer is correct.

1 The gym costs £6 per week. How much do I pay for a year?

×	50	
6	300	120

Answer: £312

2 I pay 87p for lunch every day. How much for a 65-day term?

×	80	7
60	4800	420
5		35

Answer: £59·70

3 I downloaded 47 MP3 tracks at 79p each. How much did I spend?

×	70	7
40	2800	280
9	630	

Answer: £37·13 in total

4 My phone costs £56 per month. How much will I pay over 3 years?

×	50	6
30	1500	
6	300	12

Answer: £2016

5 I bought 12 concert tickets at £112 each. How much did I pay in total?

×	100	10	2
10	1000	100	20
2	20	20	

Answer: £1344

6 I am at school for 385 minutes a day. How many minutes for 25 school days?

×	300	60	5
20	6000	1600	100
5	1500	40	

Answer: 9625 minutes

7 My job pays £4·50 per hour. How much will I earn in 15 hours?

×	4	50
10	40	500
5	20	

Answer: £67·50

8 I bought 23 CDs last year at £8·98 each. How much did I pay?

×	8	·9	·08
20	16		1·6
3	24	2·7	0·24

Answer: £206·54

eXtra Use the correct answers above and answer these using mental methods.
  1 How much could I save if I paid an annual gym subscription of £250?
  2 How much will my lunches cost me for three 65-day terms?
  3 How much extra will I have to pay if music tracks go up to 89p each?
  4 If my phone bill goes down by £5 per month, how much will I save?

Summer holiday

1 Find the cheapest summer holiday for a family of two adults and four children using this table of prices. You can choose self-catering or hotel rooms (hotel rooms include breakfast). Work out the costs and make your decision.

Hotel	Per adult: self-catering	Per adult: hotel	First child: self-catering or hotel	Each further child: self-catering or hotel
Sunny Beach	£605	£519	£329	£379
Kos View	£545	£620	£415	£395
Stelios Bay	£519	£490	£295	£450
Arta Apartments	£499	Not available	£429	£429

2 Two more adult relatives want to go too. What is the total cost now? What is your decision now – have you changed your mind?

Here are the prices of the holiday items the group needs.

	Child	Adult		Child	Adult
1 pair of shorts	£3·99	£8·99	1 book	£1·98	£3·98
1 pair of beach shoes	£3	£5	1 sunhat	£2	£4·50
1 suitcase	£22	£37	1 pair of sunglasses	£4·99	£18
1 pair of shoes	£6	£11	1 camera	£5·75	£5·75
1 wash bag	£1	£2·99	1 swimsuit	£6·50	£14·99
1 beach bag	£2·50	£7·30	1 shirt	£4·35	£7·95
1 bottle of after-sun	£3·99	£3·99	1 set of underwear	£4·99	£7·44
1 T-shirt	£1·98	£4	1 magazine	99p	£2·95
1 pair of trousers	£5·25	£12	1 beach towel	£5·80	£5·80
1 beach ball	£2·97	£2·97	1 bottle of sun-block	£3·99	£3·99

3 Use PCM 37 to calculate the total cost of the holiday shopping for both groups.

The flights are to and from London Gatwick, but the family lives in Newcastle. They have decided to get the train to the airport. Use the internet to find the cost of the cheapest rail tickets for the family. Would a railcard make the total train journey cheaper?

More money

Britain started using a decimal currency in 1971. Before that, the coins all had different names and nicknames. For example:

- a **farthing** was $\frac{1}{4}$ of a penny. It would be almost worthless now.
- a **groat** was a silver coin. It would be worth 4p now.
- a **tanner** was the name for a sixpence. It would be worth $2\frac{1}{2}$p now.
- a **bob** was the name for a shilling. It would be worth 5p now.
- a **florin** was two shillings. It would be worth 10p now.
- a **crown** was five shillings. It would be worth 25p now.
- a **guinea** was one pound, one shilling. It would be worth £1·05 now.

Nowadays in Britain, we don't have nicknames for our coins but we do have nicknames for certain amounts of money. For example:

- a **quid** (£1)
- a **score** (£20)
- a **pony** (£25)
- a **ton** (£100)
- a **monkey** (£500)
- a **grand** (£1000)

1 Work out what each of these items would cost in decimal money.

Car	Six grand, one monkey and a pony
Bicycle	3 ponies and 3 crowns
Trainers	60 guineas
Computer game	7 quid, 2 florins and a bob
TV	One score less than a monkey
Cinema Ticket	Five quid, one crown and one groat
CD	Two quid and a florin less than a score
Mobile phone	A ton and a guinea
MP3 player	Half a ton and 2 tanners
Bus fare	Five groats, a bob, a florin and a quid

2 What is the total cost of all ten items?

 Use the internet to find out more about the currency that was used in Britain before 1971. How was it different to the decimal currency? What coins were used? How were things priced?

Pop tour

The pop group The Gang are going on tour.

This table shows the date, the city, the audience attendance and the ticket price of each of their concerts.

Date	City	Attendance	Ticket price
October 24th	Glasgow	12 500	£32·50
October 25th	Newcastle	11 000	£32·50
November 4th	Sheffield	12 500	£32·50
November 5th	Manchester	19 000	£35
November 6th	Liverpool	10 600	£32·50
November 8th	Bournemouth	6500	£32·50
November 9th	Brighton	4500	£32·50
November 12th	London	23 000	£35
November 15th	Plymouth	2500	£32·50
November 16th	Nottingham	9300	£32·50
November 18th	Cardiff	5500	£32·50
November 21st	Birmingham	14 000	£35

1 Use the distance chart on PCM 39 to calculate the total number of kilometres the group will cover during their tour.

2 Use the time chart on PCM 40 to calculate the total time the group will spend travelling during their tour.

3 How many days are there between the first date and the last date of the tour?

4 How many rest days do the group have?

5 How many people in total will see the group during this tour?

6 For each city, what is the value of the tickets sold?

7 What is the total value of all the tickets sold for the whole tour?

8 Could all the money raised in ticket sales be profit?

Use the map of Britain on PCM 41 and mark on each of the cities on the tour. What order would you visit the cities in to make the shortest tour? Why? What would the total distance be? How long would be spent travelling?

Subtracting with a difference

I Think of a 3-digit number and reverse it, for example 721 and 127. Subtract the smaller number from the larger number using the negative number method.

$$
\begin{array}{r}
721 \\
- \ 127 \\
\hline
\end{array}
$$

700 – 100	=	600
20 – 20	=	00
1 – 7	=	⁻6

700 – 100 = 600
20 – 20 = 00
1 – 7 = ⁻6   **The answer is 600 – 6 = 594**

2 Reverse your answer to question I. Subtract the smaller number from the larger again, using the same method. Repeat until you can go no further.

3 Repeat with these numbers.

532   761   829   503

What do you notice? Does this happen with any 3-digit number?

4 Now think of a 4-digit number and reverse it, for example 5431 and 1345. Subtract the smaller number from the larger number.

$$
\begin{array}{r}
5431 \\
- \ 1345 \\
\hline
\end{array}
$$

5000 – 1000   4000
400 – 300   100
30 – 40   –10
1 – 5   – 4   **The answer is 4000 + 100 – 10 – 4 = 4086**

5 Reverse your answer to question 4. Subtract the smaller number from the larger number. Repeat until you can go no further.

6 Repeat with these numbers.

4152   6375   7856

What do you notice? Does this happen with any 4-digit number?

7 What happens with the numbers 2746 and 6472? Can you find any other numbers with this property?

e**X**tra

Explore what happens with decimal numbers such as:
63·2 and 2·36   87·9 and 9·78   6·59 and 95·6   91·82 and 28·19
You may use a calculator.

Making a bird table

Wood is measured using length by width by depth.
This can be shortened to l × w × d.

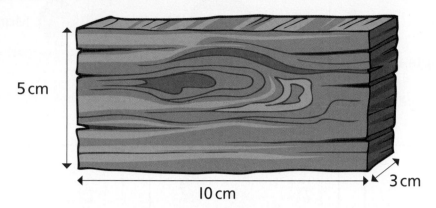

5 cm

10 cm

3 cm

For example this piece of wood is 10 cm long, 5 cm wide and 3 cm deep.

Matthew, Asha, Leigh, Emma and Tariq
have decided to make a bird table.

Look at the instructions on PCM 42 to see
what pieces of wood the children will need
to buy to make their bird table.

The children must buy the full-sized pieces
of wood from the hardware shop.

1 Use the size information and price list on
PCM 42 to calculate how much it costs to
build one bird table.

The children decide they would like to build
a bird table each.

2 Calculate how much it costs to build five
bird tables.

Remember you might be able to make more
than one piece from a full-sized piece of wood.

3 How much does one bird table cost to build if you build five bird tables at once?

Look at the dimensions on PCM 42. How much of each type of wood
is left over after building one bird table? How much wood is left
over after building five bird tables?

How much juice?

Apple   Tomato   Strawberry

Banana   Lemon   Melon   Mango

Pineapple   Pear   Orange

1 Work out how much juice each fruit makes when it is juiced.

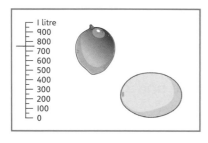

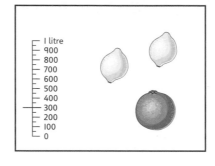

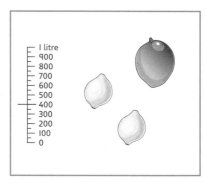

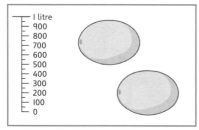

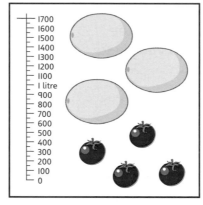

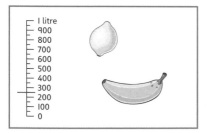

eXtra

If you juiced one of each fruit together how much juice would you get in total?
Choose three different fruits you would like to mix together. Decide how many of each you would like. How much juice could you make?

Dice probabilities

> What would happen if you threw two dice 100 times and found the total of the two dice numbers each time?
> Is there an equal chance of getting each possible total from 2 to 12?

1 Throw two dice 100 times. Record the scores in a tally chart.

2 What happens? How can you explain this?

3 Copy and complete the table showing the total score each time.

+		First dice					
		1	2	3	4	5	6
Second dice	1						
	2						
	3						
	4						
	5						
	6						

4 Which total occurs most frequently? Least frequently?

5 What are the chances of throwing a total of 3?

6 What are the chances of throwing a total of 8?

7 What are the chances of getting a double?

8 Which is more likely, a total of 4 or a total of 10?

9 Which is more likely, an odd or an even number?

10 Which is more likely, a multiple of 3 or a multiple of 4?

11 Draw a bar graph showing the possible scores. What pattern do you see?

eXtra What would happen if the two dice were multiplied? Draw up a table showing the possible outcomes. Answer questions 4–10 for multiplying.

Fruity pie charts

36 children voted whether they preferred oranges, apples, cherries, bananas or plums. This pie chart shows the results.

Survey of 36 children's favourite fruit

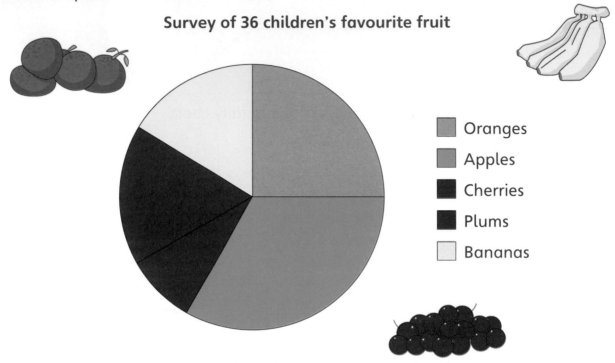

Oranges
Apples
Cherries
Plums
Bananas

I How many children chose each fruit?

2 In another survey of 180 children, 45 chose oranges, 30 chose apples, 20 chose cherries, 30 chose plums and 55 chose bananas. Draw a pie chart to show this information.

> What do you notice about the size of the slices for each fruit in your pie chart, compared with the first pie chart?

3 Why is the slice for apples smaller on the second chart even though more people in the second survey liked apples?

4 Why is the slice for oranges the same on both charts?

5 What can you say about the other fruits?

eXtra Do a class survey of favourite fruits and draw a pie chart.
Why would it be helpful if there were 30 children in the survey?

Fences

You have 40 fence panels each I metre wide. You are going to use these to make an enclosed space in the shape of an L.

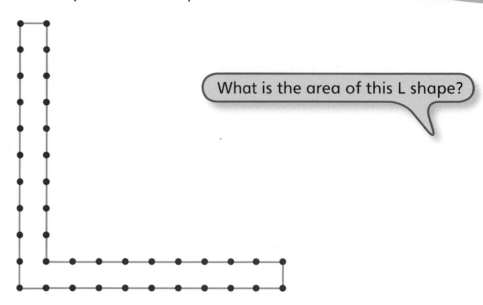

What is the area of this L shape?

I What is the largest L-shaped area that can be enclosed by the fencing?

2 What would be the largest L-shaped area if you had I00 fence panels?

Now think about using the 40 fence panels to make a T shape.

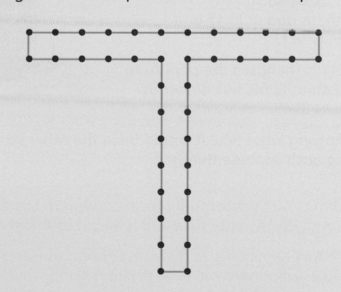

3 Would the area inside the T shape be as big as the area inside the L shape?

eXtra What would the largest area be inside an F or an E shape made using 40 fence panels?

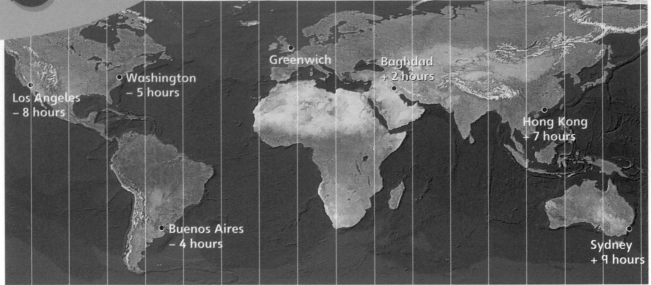

Greenwich

Baghdad
+ 2 hours

Los Angeles
– 8 hours

Washington
– 5 hours

Hong Kong
+ 7 hours

Buenos Aires
– 4 hours

Sydney
+ 9 hours

At different times of the year the difference between Greenwich Mean Time and times in other countries is not always the same. In summer we put our clocks forward an hour, but some other countries don't.

Jevan lives in Manchester.
One Saturday he gets up at 08:30.
He goes shopping with his dad at 10:45 and has lunch with his family at 13:15.

He plays football with his friends in the park from 15:20 to 16:45, has a bath at 18:00, has dinner at 19:30 and goes to bed at 21:45.

1 Draw up a table showing what time it would be in the other six cities on the map when Jevan is doing each of these things.

2 It takes roughly 13 hours 40 minutes to fly from London to Los Angeles. If the plane leaves London at 06:54, what time will it be in Los Angeles when it arrives?

3 It takes roughly 12 hours 10 minutes to fly from London to Hong Kong. If the plane leaves London at 17:02, what time will it be in Hong Kong when it arrives?

4 Make up some questions like these and give them to a partner to solve.

e**X**tra

Not all cities are an exact number of hours ahead of or behind Greenwich Mean Time. Find what time it would be for the different events in Jevan's day in Mumbai (+5:30), Darwin (+9:30) and Caracas (–7:30).

Metric time

Many people have suggested different time units based on metric time, to replace the days, hours, minutes and seconds that we use today. In March 1794 Joseph Louis Lagrange, who was involved in developing the metric system, proposed the French names *déci-jour* and *centi-jour*. This translates as deciday and centiday in English.

People have suggested units for decimal divisions of the day such as $\frac{1}{10}$, $\frac{1}{100}$, $\frac{1}{1000}$ or $\frac{1}{100\,000}$ of a day. Other divisions such as $\frac{1}{20}$ or $\frac{1}{40}$ of a day have also been put forward with names such as tick, meck, chi, chron and moment. These units have been combined into multiples with metric prefixes such as centi and kilo. These alternative time units have not been accepted and not many people have heard of them.

In 1897 a commission for the decimalisation of time was set up by the French Bureau of Longitude. They proposed using the standard hour as the base unit of metric time, but the idea did not catch on and it was rejected.

1 Invent your own system of metric time units. You could use one of the ideas above or make up your own. Give your units names.

A day will still be the same length of time, but instead of hours, minutes and seconds you should break it into units based on multiples of 10.

2 Use your new units to draw up a typical timetable for your day at school.

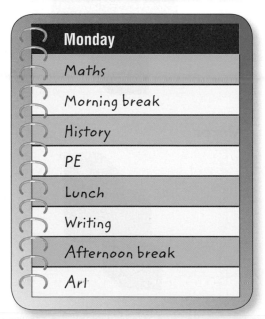

Monday

Maths

Morning break

History

PE

Lunch

Writing

Afternoon break

Art

Do you think your new system of time units would be easier to use than the one we have now?

 eXtra We group the number of days into weeks, months and years. What would a metric year look like?

Reflecting 3D shapes

What will the reflection of each of these shapes look like?

Make theses shapes using linking cubes.
Predict what the reflection of each shape will look like.
Reflect each shape in a mirror, as shown, and sketch the reflection that you see as accurately as you can. Was your prediction correct?

1 Mirror

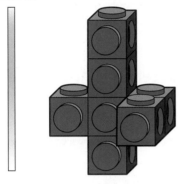

2 Mirror

3 Mirror

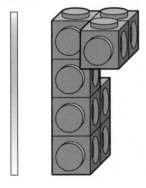

4 Mirror

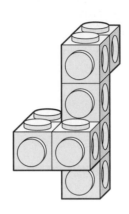

5 Mirror

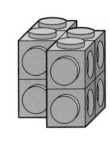

6 Mirror

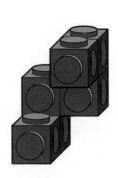

eXtra Make up your own 3D shapes. Predict their reflections then look at them in a mirror.

Transformations in patterns

Celtic pattern

Islamic pattern

Roman mosaic pattern

What transformations can you see in the patterns?

1 Use mirrors and tracing paper to identify the different rotational symmetries, reflective symmetries and translations in each pattern.

2 Write a short summary of your findings.

Choose your favourite pattern on this page and make your own version of it that uses different transformations.

Exploring division

Before you try a division, look to see if you can simplify it by dividing both the numbers by the same number.

Example I

	$702 \div 18 =$
Dividing both numbers by 2 gives:	$351 \div 9 =$
Dividing both numbers by 3 gives:	$117 \div 3 = 39$

Use this method to find answers to these questions:

I $336 \div 16 =$ **2** $608 \div 32 =$ **3** $864 \div 24 =$

4 $1736 \div 28 =$ **5** $945 \div 27 =$

6 Check each answer using standard written methods.

Is this method always helpful?

The quotient is 45.
The divisor is a number between 22 and 40.
What is the dividend?

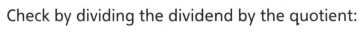
dividend ÷ divisor = quotient

Example 2

	$? \div \ ? = 45$
You can start from:	$90 \div \ 2 = 45$
Multiplying both numbers by 3 gives:	$270 \div \ 6 = 45$
Multiplying both numbers by 3 again gives:	$810 \div 18 = 45$
Multiplying both numbers by 2 gives:	$1620 \div 36 = 45$

Check by dividing the dividend by the quotient:

```
        40
        36
  45)1620
     1350      30 × 45
     ─────
     −270
     −270      6 × 45
     ─────
        0
```

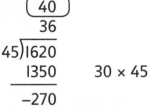

Use this method to find answers to these questions.
Five numbers have each been divided by a different number between 22 and 40.
The quotients are below. What might each division question have been?

7 26   **8** 51   **9** 62   **10** 67   **11** 83

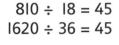
e**X**tra   Investigate if division questions with decimals can be solved like this.

Missing-number divisions

Find numbers to put in the boxes to make the divisions work.
Write out each division. Check your answers using standard
written methods.

1 ☐☐☐ ÷ ☐ = 26

2 ☐☐☐ ÷ ☐ = 17

3 ☐☐☐ ÷ ☐ = 32 r 7

4 ☐☐☐ ÷ ☐ = 19 r 5

5 ☐☐☐☐ ÷ ☐ = 351

6 ☐☐☐☐ ÷ ☐ = 136 r 29

7 ☐☐☐ ÷ ☐ = 41

8 ☐☐ ÷ ☐ = 33

9 ☐☐☐ ÷ ☐ = 18 r2

10 ☐☐☐ ÷ ☐☐ = 41 r6

What methods did you use to
find possible missing numbers?

 e**X**tra

☐☐☐ ÷ ☐ = 27

Copy out this missing-number division. Use a 1–9 spinner.
Spin the spinner four times and place the digits in the boxes.
You can choose which box to put each digit in. How close
can you get to the target number 27?

Long division

$$
\begin{array}{r}
\boxed{4 \cdot 3} \\
4 \cdot 26 \\
23\overline{)97 \cdot 98} \\
-92 \qquad 4 \times 23 \\
\hline
5 \cdot 98 \\
-4 \cdot 6 \qquad 0 \cdot 2 \times 23 \\
\hline
1 \cdot 38 \\
-1 \cdot 38 \qquad 0 \cdot 06 \times 23
\end{array}
$$

Use this method to solve these divisions, estimating first.

1 $91 \cdot 63 \div 17 =$ **2** $90 \cdot 72 \div 28 =$

3 $148 \cdot 68 \div 42 =$ **4** $194 \cdot 06 \div 31 =$

Solve these word problems. Estimate first, then work out exactly how much each person pays. Round your answers to the nearest penny. Check your answers using multiplication.

5 Who pays more, eight people sharing a bill for £94·75 or 13 people sharing a bill for £152·80?

6 Who pays more, 12 people sharing a bill for £106·50 or 15 people sharing a bill for £128·65?

7 Who pays more, 16 people sharing a bill for £251·45 or 22 people sharing a bill for £346·05?

eXtra

Your class wins the Headteacher's Challenge, a prize of £920·50. This is shared between all the children, who each donate their share to their favourite charity. How much will you each donate, rounded to the nearest penny?

Angel of the North

The Angel of the North is a large steel sculpture just outside Gateshead. It was put up in 1998 and cost £800 000. The artist Antony Gormley used a model of his own body for the Angel's body. The sculpture is 20 m high and almost 54 m wide. The Angel's body weighs 100 tonnes and the wings weigh 50 tonnes each, making it 200 tonnes in total. This steel could make 16 double-decker buses. The Angel was built to last at least 100 years.

In 2008 a 2 m high scale model of the Angel was sold for £2 280 000. A smaller model which is approximately $\frac{1}{20}$ of the size of the original has been valued at £1 000 000.

1 If the real Angel was sold, how much do you think it would cost based on the models? Explain how you decided.

2 How tall (to nearest cm) is the smaller model?

3 How wide (to nearest cm) are the wings on each of the scale models?

4 What proportion of the large sculpture is the 2 m high sculpture?

5 The statue of Nelson at the top of Nelson's column is 5·25 m tall. A model of Nelson is 2·1 m tall. How many times bigger is the statue than the model?

6 The statue of Nelson weighs approximately 18 tonnes. How much should the model weigh?

7 The London Eye is 135 m high. If I made a model of it $\frac{1}{50}$ of its original size, how tall would my model be?

8 The 'Eye' weighs 2100 tonnes. How much would my scale model weigh?

I buy a model of the Eiffel Tower that is $\frac{1}{650}$ of its size. The real tower is 324 m high. How tall (to the nearest cm) is my model? If my model was 1 m tall, what would be the proportion of the model to the real tower?

Maps

Look at the maps on PCM 49.
Map 1 shows the shape of the roads.
Map 2 shows the roads as straight lines.

> 1 km is 100 000 cm.
> 1 mile is 63 360 inches.

The map scales are shown as ratios. You can use these to calculate real distances in metric or imperial measures.

Look at Map 1.

The scale of 1:140 000 means that a measurement of 1 cm on Map 1 is 140 000 cm in real life. That is 1·4 km.

It also means that a measurement of 1 inch on Map 1 is 140 000 inches in real life. That is approximately 2·2 miles.

How far is it to the nearest kilometre between each pair of towns?

1 West Auckland to Bishop Auckland

2 Hunwick to Willington

3 Coundon to Shildon

4 Shildon to Spennymoor

Look at Map 2.

5 Plan the shortest route from Leeds to Macclesfield. Will you go via Wakefield or via Halifax? Measure the lengths of roads on this map and convert them to the real distance using the scale.

6 You have to travel from Oldham to Chesterfield. Which route will be the shortest distance?

eXtra   Find at least three different scale maps of your local area. Find a journey you might make and use the scale for each of the maps to calculate the distances. How accurate are each of the different maps?

Three ratios

Jaz, Amit and Ellie are sharing a picnic.

1 Ellie gets $\frac{2}{5}$ of the chocolate. How many pieces does she get?

Bar of chocolate: 20 pieces

2 Jaz gets $\frac{1}{4}$. How many pieces?

3 The rest goes to Amit. What proportion of the whole bar does he get?

4 Copy and complete the ratio. 8:5:?

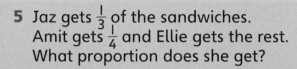

5 Jaz gets $\frac{1}{3}$ of the sandwiches. Amit gets $\frac{1}{4}$ and Ellie gets the rest. What proportion does she get?

12 sandwiches

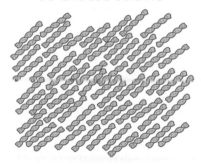

6 How many sandwiches do they each get?

7 What is the ratio?

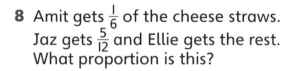

8 Amit gets $\frac{1}{6}$ of the cheese straws. Jaz gets $\frac{5}{12}$ and Ellie gets the rest. What proportion is this?

60 cheese straws

9 How many cheese straws does each person get?

10 What is the ratio?

11 Ellie gets $\frac{1}{3}$ of the orange drink. Jaz gets $\frac{2}{5}$ and Amit gets the rest. What proportion does he get?

Orange drink 150 cl

12 How much do they each get?

13 What is the ratio in its lowest terms?

 eXtra

Draw your own fraction models for the following items and find the third proportion for each one.
- 18 sweets: two of the shares are $\frac{1}{3}$ and $\frac{1}{6}$.
- 30 marshmallows: two of the shares are $\frac{3}{10}$ and $\frac{1}{3}$.

Domino rectangles

You are going to make rectangles using dominoes.
The rectangles must always be two squares high.

With a single domino,
there is only one possible
arrangement.

A pair of dominoes can
be arranged in two
ways.

With three dominoes
these two arrangements
can be made.
More are possible.

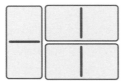 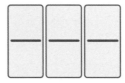

1 What other arrangements can be made with three dominoes?

2 Try to find all the arrangements for four dominoes.

3 Investigate arrangements with five dominoes.

4 Copy and complete this table.

Number of dominoes	1	2	3	4	5	6	7
Number of arrangements	1	2					

5 What patterns can you see? How many arrangements would there be for nine dominoes? How did you work this out?

 e**X**tra

Look at these arrangements of dominoes, with the dots.

This is the smallest possible total for two dominoes.

This is the largest possible total for two dominoes.

Find the smallest and largest possible totals for all of your arrangements.

PINs

> What is a PIN? Do you know anyone who has one?
> What do you know about PINs?

Each of these children has a special way of remembering their four-digit PIN.

Match each child with their PIN. There will be five PINs left over.

1

My PIN is the sum of the first 11 prime numbers, multiplied by 10.

My PIN is two 2-digit square numbers.

2

3

My PIN is a cubed number.

The first two digits of my PIN are the sum of all the factors of 24. The second two digits are the sum of all the factors of 36.

4

5

The prime factors of my PIN are the first four odd prime numbers.

My PIN is a square number.

6

7

My PIN is the first four prime numbers in reverse.

My PIN is the sum of the first 15 square numbers.

8

9

My PIN is the first 4-digit prime number.

My PIN is two 2-digit prime numbers, less than 30.

10

PINs

2327   1240   2436   1001   1600   9753   6091

1009

5050   2500   8164   1155   5321   7532

1331

 Extra Make up five PINs of your own. Write number facts you could use to remember them.